Sea Kayaking in Florida

2nd Edition

David and Mark
Gluckman

Pineapple Press, Inc.
Sarasota, Florida

Inquiries should be addressed to:

Pineapple Press, Inc.
P.O. Box 3889
Sarasota, Florida 34230
www.pineapplepress.com

Library of Congress Cataloging-in-Publication Data

Gluckman, David.
  Sea kayaking in Florida / by David Gluckman.— 2nd ed.
      p. cm.
  Includes bibliographical references and index.
  ISBN 1-56164-322-X (pb : alk. paper)
  1. Sea kayaking—Florida—Guidebooks. 2. Florida—Guidebooks. I. Title.

  GV788.5.G58 2004
  797.1'224'09759—dc22

                                                      2004015582

Second Edition
10 9 8 7 6 5 4 3 2 1

Design by Ramonda Talkie
Printed in the United States of America

DISCLAIMER: Most of the literature on kayaking contains a great deal of information that's useless for Florida. The reason for this is that sea kayaks were developed by Eskimos for cold water and most experienced kayakers come from England, the Northwest or the Northeast. Paddlers from these harsher climes face special conditions that are rarely present in Florida. These special conditions often dictate the types of equipment they need and safety precautions they should take. If you follow the recommendations written by and about these paddlers, you would be very safe while kayaking in Florida. Unfortunately, you may not be very comfortable. This book attempts to introduce the Florida experience into the equation. It's a "kinder, gentler" book because of "kinder, gentler" weather and boating conditions. However, in order to avoid lawsuits, I recommend that you take every single precaution recommended for the worst possible conditions imaginable any place in the world. If you do not, you are accepting the risks you undertake.

Contents

Color photo pages appear between pp. 86 and 87

Chapter 9 Weather Patterns and Tides ⌣·⎯ 87

Chapter 10 Coastal Critters for Enjoyment
and Pain ⌣·⎯ 96

Introduction
to the First Edition

This book is about a special type of boat in a special kind of place. It's a boat that's safe and fun to paddle and a place that sings to you with soft breezes and gentle waves. The boat brings you close to what you want to see and the place lets you enjoy those sights in relative comfort. The sea kayak is not a whitewater kayak and Florida is not Alaska, but the enjoyment can equal both if you do it in the right place at the right time of the year.

The nicest thing about a sea kayak is that it's generally stable and wants to go straight. It's a safe boat for most paddlers. Wind and big waves don't bother it much, and you can close it up and stay dry when the weather changes. The more proficient you are, the more proficient it is. The first solo Atlantic Ocean crossing in a sea kayak was accomplished in the early 1900s. That boat was 21' long and shaped much like the modern sea kayak. A recent sea kayak crossing (22' modern fiberglass boat) was made from the San Francisco area to Hawaii in 60 days.

This book isn't about Atlantic or Pacific Ocean crossings. It's about the safe and lazy paddling in Florida. It's written for the novice who wants to get into the sport as well as experienced paddlers who want some guidance on what gear to use, what weather conditions to expect and new places to paddle and camp. Since more kayaks than canoes are purchased each year (and women buy more than half), you can expect to find a greater number of your friends in non-motorized craft on salt water than ever before. There is no better way to explore the coast of Florida than in a sea kayak, so read on, shove off and enjoy!

Introduction
to the Second Edition

It's been almost ten years since I started writing the first edition of Sea Kayaking in Florida, and both the publisher and I figured it was about time for a revision. Though the basic technology hasn't changed much (for about two thousand years) there have been a lot of incremental advances that are worth writing about. In addition, the paddling trail concept has gotten better governmental support and more specific maps and locations have been developed. With the help of my brother, Mark, who kindly agreed to co-author the Big Bend Sea Grasses Paddling trail portion of this revised version, you'll find a wealth of new information that we hope will make your paddling in Florida safer and more enjoyable. I've updated boat and paddle specifications along with GPS coordinates for much of the Big Bend trail and its campsites. I've also updated some of the livery information in the index with appropriate websites (which didn't exist when the first edition came out) as well as many other parts of the original book. Fair winds and smooth seas to you all.

—*David Gluckman, Fall 2004*

Acknowledgment

This book could never have been written without the support and gentle prodding of my wife Casey, who made me paddle when I got lazy and never interfered with my buying habits so I wouldn't interfere with hers. Many thanks to the enthusiastic support of all my paddling friends, especially Joel Gottlieb and Mary Allgire, who were always willing to go at a moment's notice even though they never knew where we would end up. A special thanks to Sam Lamar of Tallahassee's Canoe Shop, who got us started in sea kayaking, fed us an endless supply of new high-tech goodies, and picked us up when we were done. Without them this book would not have happened.

Chapter 1

BOATS

I t's always good to start at the top of the want list. You need a boat. Actually, you need a sea kayak if you want the most enjoyment from paddling Florida's coastal waters. Sure, you can see much of Florida in a canoe most of the time. But when the wind is in your face, or quartering off the bow at 20 knots, you'd probably be better off swimming than trying to paddle a canoe. The most recent statistics on canoe sales reflect this new understanding. Since 1992, kayaks have out-sold canoes in this country 60% to 40%.

A sea kayak is a very special craft. It was invented for hunting near the icy Arctic and to support people safely over long distances in rough water. It's much longer than it is wide and glides through the water with little energy. It's like a squashed canoe with a top on it. There are a couple of hundred different models sold commercially today in all different sizes, shapes, colors, and prices. (See Illustration # 1-1. Various Sea Kayaks.)

With all these potential boats which is the best for Florida? You probably won't get two paddlers in the state to agree on any one boat. (That's why you can justify that second — or third — boat to your spouse after the addiction sets in). However, there are better kayaks for Florida and Florida conditions than others. This chapter will discuss the boats and what you should consider when buying your own.

Illustration # 1-1. Various Sea Kayaks

1. Shapes/Sizes

Sea kayaks come in many shapes and sizes. There are high-performance, long, skinny greyhounds that speed through the water like needlefish, turn over when you least expect it, and carry only camping gear that fits into tubes no larger than 2' long and 8" in diameter. There are also mailboat-type clunkers that are wide, very stable, slow, and have enough carrying space to take your medium cooler and double-burner Coleman. Florida conditions allow either type to be used safely, so your choice becomes more economic and personal than safety-related.

My preference is a wider boat (23" to 25") rather a narrow (17" to 22"), faster boat as long as it's at least 14' long. (Note: Boat speed is basically determined by a mathematical formula that multiplies the length times the width. The longer and narrower, the faster the boat.) Speed has rarely been important to me. I don't plan long days and the difference over 10 to 15 miles is usually not that important. Since wider boats are generally more comfortable, carry larger loads and are more stable, the lack of speed is rarely a factor to consider when buying your first boat. Now, my second boat will be one of those greyhounds. They're so beautiful!

The primary functional shape you should consider for Florida is a boat that will track well in reasonable winds. This means that it will keep a straight line while being paddled with a wind blowing across the boat. The part of boat design that controls tracking is generally the keel. The keel is the part of the boat below the waterline that runs longitudinally down the center of the bottom. It extends down slightly from the bottom from one end to the other. In some sea kayaks it's a crease, in others a real projection of 1/4" or more. If you install a rudder or skeg (see Section 3 of this chapter for details and arguments about rudders), there should be little concern about this feature. However, there are some sea kayaks that track too well and will cause trouble if you want to do anything but go straight. The fixed-skeg Nordkap is a good example. Its turning radius is close to that of a super tanker: not very good for the occasional freshwater river or lake. On the other hand, there are boats with no real keel that require a lot of rudder foot pressure all the time.

There are some boats called sea kayaks that are really glorified river boats. They're usually cheaper than most, shorter in length, have flat or rounded bottoms and cannot be fitted with rudders. They will handle wind and roughish water with a lot of experience and muscle but can be pretty daunting for the beginner. People who start out in these boats rarely become sea kayakers (or rarely become very good sea kayakers).

Manufacturers make sea kayaks in many styles and shapes. Read the annual buying guide in *Canoe and Kayak* magazine for a description of the various configurations. Some have high raked (upward pointy) bows that will help you get out on floating ice (a real need for Florida?). Some have chisel bows (straight up and down) and raked sterns that are better in head winds than tail winds. Those with raked bows and chisel sterns are better in tail winds than head winds. Unless the winds or waves always come from the same direction you need to get a boat that compromises, one that won't be too bad in any direction. (See Illustration # 1-2. General Shapes.) Don't worry too much about any of this. Kayakers are great ego trippers and one method of ego massage is to discuss esoterica about boat design that few really understand.

In Florida, any boat that's truly a sea kayak will do fine. The only real criteria for Florida should be comfort level. Can you sit in the boat for more than 20 minutes at a time without your legs going to sleep and your back going into spasm? Rule 1 through 100 of boat buying is, try it first. Paddle it more than an hour without getting out. If it still feels okay, it's probably a good first boat.

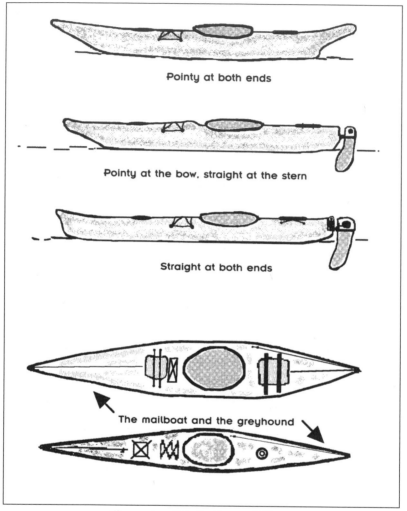

Pointy at both ends

Pointy at the bow, straight at the stern

Straight at both ends

The mailboat and the greyhound

Illustration # 1-2. General Shapes

2. Materials

Kayaks are usually made from four types of materials. The lightest and most expensive is fiberglass (including high-tech materials like Kevlar and graphite which can double the price). Today these boats are referred to as "composite" boats, usually because of the mixing of fiberglass and other fibers. Composite boats are generally the fastest but tend to be more brittle than the others. The earliest of the Northwest Coast modern boats were made out of fiberglass and most made out there today continue the tradition. You don't sit on them, drop them from your car or crash into rocks with them unless you have a lot of duct tape handy. A boat for one person can weigh from 35 to 60 pounds and a double from 65 to 110 pounds.

The cheapest and often heaviest material is a form of polymer or plastic resin, the earliest form of which was a type of polyethylene of one form or another. Nicknamed "heavy Tupperware," it's the waxy-feeling, flexible material now being used for almost all whitewater kayaks. They are made by pouring plastic granules or powder into a mold, heating and spinning the mold until all the crevasses are filled up. The process, usually called "rotomolding" was a revolutionary discovery when it was made in the 1970s. These boats are a little clunky, but durable, with a lot of "give" on impact. You can usually pick the boat up and put it right back on the car after the bungee cords fail at 55 m.p.h.. The bottom peels a little when you scrunch over the hidden oyster bars, but otherwise it's almost indestructible in normal situations. The advertised weight (usually somewhat lighter than actual weight for some unknown reason) for a boat for one person is from 48 to 65 pounds, depending on the model.

Over the last few years some of these plastic resin processes (producing what are now all lumped together as "plastic" boats) have made huge advances over their earlier, clunky cousins. The thickness and weights have been reduced and the durability increased. The newest type replaces the rotomolding process by forming boats from large sheets of plastic heated and vacuumed into place. Plastic boats are by far the best selling boats on the market because of their price and versatility.

The third type is made from wood with fiberglass or epoxy coverings. There are a few commercially made (try Pigmy Boats in Port Townsend, Washington, for complete boats or kits), but most of these are of the homemade variety. They look so good I'd be afraid to put them in the water. These are not necessarily recommended for Florida (unless you make it yourself and can't afford one of the others) because of the sun's impact on the finish and the oyster and sand impact on the bottom.

The fourth type is skin boats. These are so specialized today that I've never tried one. The original kayaks were all skin boats, usually made from unwilling seals. The newer skin boats are canvas with a rubberized coating, a form of flexible plastic or inflatable plastic tubes. Most of these are folding boats that can be dismantled for shipping. I know someone who has one, but it's been folded up in the attic for longer than I've known her and hasn't come down yet. I looked at these boats before I bought my others. They were too expensive, too heavy, too easily punctured and basically impractical for my needs in Florida.

3. Rudders/Skegs

Rudders are movable flat pieces of metal affixed to the stern of the boat that can be steered from the cockpit to control the direction of the boat's movement. Control is almost always with the feet (it's hard to paddle and steer with your hands at the same time). Skegs are rudders that don't move from side to side but can be either fixed in place or raised from or lowered into the water. (See Illustrations # 1-3a & b. Rudder and Skeg.)

The rudder and mobile skeg can be raised and lowered by a deck line that stretches from the rudder to the cockpit. Some boat manufacturers claim their boats have built-in skegs as part of the boat design. I guess they do, but they don't seem to be as effective as the detached ones. The purpose of each is supposed to be the same: to counteract the effects of wind (and sometimes currents) on the boat so that it can go in the direction you want without your having to break up your paddling symmetry to counteract the wind's effects. Without a rudder or skeg of some sort, a wind from the front quarter will cause most boats to turn toward the direction

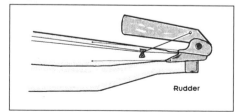

Illustration # 1-3a. Rudder *Illustration # 1-3b. Skeg*

the wind is blowing. To counteract this, you have to paddle more (or harder) on one side than the other in order to go straight. Double-bladed kayak paddles don't like to do that. Backs, shoulders, and side muscles don't like this either.

For years there was a great debate about the use of rudders and movable skegs on sea kayaks. The old pros were usually purists who looked at rudders with disdain (and 30-mile days and 30-m.p.h. head winds with glee). Since the early rudder systems had a tendency to fall off under those conditions, it's understandable why they were not universally supported. The old lore was that if you were good enough to paddle a sea kayak, then by golly, you were tough enough to counteract all of nature's forces with the muscles God gave you and there was no need for crutches. Of course, it was stupid statements like this that kept most people out of sea kayaks until they developed rudders and skegs.

First, let's do away with skegs. They were okay when rudders were unreliable, but they only perform half of what a rudder will do. Since you can't turn a skeg to adjust for wind direction, you still have to "overpaddle" to compensate for certain wind strengths and direction. The last time I paddled in 20-knot quartering winds with someone who had a skeg on his boat, his back went out and he bought a new boat shortly after his return. The new boat has a rudder on it. Don't buy a boat with a skeg for Florida if a rudder is available. It won't handle the variable windy conditions you sometimes find.

The new aluminum rudder kits for most sea kayaks are very good. Some rudders come out of the water and stick out behind the boat and others do a 270-degree rotation and end up pointing toward the cockpit. The latter one is nicer, but I haven't used that type enough to get attached to it. They work as advertised, are easy to maintain and don't break under normal use.

Do you need a rudder? It depends on how strong a paddler you are, what wind conditions you expect to meet, what use you intend to make of your boat and how lazy you want to be. I like the rudders on my boats. I keep them up in the river and put them down in the ocean unless I want a little more speed. (Sea kayaks are slower with the rudder down. There is a surprising amount of extra drag from a rudder, depending on its shape and size.) For me, the primary benefit of a rudder is, first and foremost, to keep the boat moving in the line I chose under adverse wind conditions. The secondary benefit is to allow me to steer the boat without paddling when I want to get close to wildlife. If you don't expect to find yourself in those situations, don't buy one unless you can think of some other reason (they look sooo cool!).

The downside to rudders is that they slow the boat down and always seem to be in the way when you carry the boat or try to put it away. They also break from time to time. You can also use them to steer too much and avoid learning important paddling skills. It's your call.

4. Cockpits/Wave Skis/Hatches/Bulkheads

The enclosed cockpit of the sea kayak is one of its greatest safety and comfort features. When the waves start breaking over the side of a canoe, it fills up, turns over and is as useful as wreck debris. When waves break over the side of a well-prepared sea kayak, the water slides off and you bob back up like a cork and go on your way, (If you forget your skirt and the cockpit fills up, it's worse than wreck debris.)

Sea kayaks are made with many different types of cockpits and humans are made in many different shapes and sizes. Sometimes they fit, sometimes they don't. Some sea kayaks, like Wave Skis, have no enclosed cockpits but are made for on-top sitting and self bailing of overflow water. I'll discuss these later in the chapter.

Your average cockpit contains a seat, seat back and access to rudder peddles or foot braces. Some also have thigh braces so that you can better stabilize the boat with your legs and have more control when you roll (IF you roll. More about this later). The long, skinny, fast boats have narrow, small cockpits. The slow, fat boats have bigger cockpits. Some double kayaks have double cockpits of various sizes and some a long single cockpit. Very large people may want to buy a double for the extra-large cockpit (doubles are discussed in Section 5).

In addition to cockpit size, seats and seat backs are very important. Describing the types won't do you any good. Put your rear end in one and try it. That's the only way to find what fits you. Be a little leery of the contoured seat bottoms where the upraised edges under your thighs can cut off circulation during long paddles. Kayak designers must have gone to special torture schools to learn how to design seat backs. There were no comfortable backs when I bought my first boat nine years ago, so I made my own (see Appendix 1 for a short course in seat back self construction). Things are getting better with the newer boats.

The reason seat backs in sea kayaks are usually so uncomfortable is that most were designed for whitewater boats that have to be able to roll easily and often. I want a seat back that gives higher support for my back than is usually provided by the manufacturer, and I don't care about rolling. If you paddle much in Florida, rolling probably won't be important to you either. From my perspective, the one critical aspect of a seat back is that you have to be able to get your skirt over it when you need to. If the skirt will fit, the only other concern is comfort. In the last year or so, I bought a Crazy-Creek™ sling-type chair that fits fairly well in both of my boats and can be taken out when I get to the beach for clean and comfortable sitting. It may be a good substitute seat back (and seat bottom) for some of you.

Since the first edition of this book was written, a number of new seat backs have come on the market as ad-ons, and new kayaks are being sold with more seat sizes and shapes to choose from. Some of these are even inflatable with waterproof plush coverings. Most have numerous adjustments in both height and thickness. Try them out and ask for something else if you like the boat but not the seat. Many dealers will work with you to get a comfortable seat rather than lose your sale.

Though I have never paddled one, the Wave Ski™ boat (see Illustration # 1-4. Wave Skis) looks like a nice fun boat for doing Florida surf and hot-weather day trips. One version of the sit-upon boat, these boats have below-deck storage, but the paddler sits on the top of a molded seat in a cockpit depression that does not access the inside of the boat. If you go over, you turn it right side up and get back on. There is little or no bailing because the water runs off through scuppers or channels. Most come with foot straps and rudders. They're more popular in Hawaii and big California surf than any place else but I see an increased usage in Florida as well. I like the protection of the enclosed boats as well as the greater storage room and stability, but there are some real advantages to sit-upon boats for short trips and surf play. In the last ten years almost every manufacturer of standard sea kayaks has introduced some form of sit-upon kayak. There is even one out there with a clear plastic bottom for under-sea viewing.

Illustration # 1-4. Wave Skis

Hatches are those openings through the deck of the kayak that let you into the inside compartments. The type of hatch on a sea kayak has very little to do with how the boat handles but a lot to do with sea worthiness and camping ease. Hatches that leak in rough seas can be very bad business. Not only can your boat fill up with water and become unmanageable, but also your gear gets all wet. In Florida, this is rarely a problem because you can usually plan not to be in rough seas if your boat or skills are not up to it. I've never had a problem with leaky hatches. That doesn't mean my hatches haven't leaked, it's just that they didn't cause a problem. This is important because some people will buy a boat because of its super-safe hatches. When they discover how uncomfortable the boat is for long trips, it spends most of its time turned over in the back yard. A lot of money for a banana-shaped grass killer! As far as I can tell, there are no commercially made boats generally available whose hatches are not acceptable. These include the neoprene covers or neoprene and hard covers of most of the "Tupperware" boats as well as the nicely tube-gasketed hard covers with twist clips on the good fiberglass models. (See Illustration # 1-5. Hatches.)

Illustration # 1-5. Hatches

The best and safest hatch covers are stupid for Florida. These are the 8″-diameter rubber covers secured with steel rings. I know someone who swears by them even as he explains how they blew off his boat in the hot sun one day because they were so tight. He's also never used his boat for camping because the holes are too small to bring the gear he needs. These boats are a prime example of cross-Atlantic expedition engineering for the needs of cross-bay weekenders. You'll usually find them on the more expensive greyhounds but they occasionally show up on some of the less expensive boats from time to time. If you never plan to camp, it probably won't matter. If you do, forget anything but hatches with reasonable openings so that you can access what you want with a minimum of effort. (Note: The newer boats with the small, round hatches avoid blowoff problems by drilling pin holes in the bulkheads or covers. This lets out the superheated air without exploding the boat. If you buy an older model, drill a pin hole or two. It won't, however, solve the gear loading problems.)

Bulkheads are the closures that seal off the kayak to form watertight compartments (forward and aft and sometimes in the middle) that are accessible only through the deck hatches. They are important for safety and camping. The safety reason is to keep water that gets into the boat through the cockpit from filling up the boat and sinking it or making it too difficult to paddle. With good bulkheads, a boat that turns over and fills with water will still float and continue to be seaworthy enough to allow it to be pumped out while you sit in it. For camping purposes, bulkheads theoretically (and sometimes actually) keep your gear safe and dry below the howling seas. Bulkheads usually work fine for safety purposes and sometimes for camping.

Fiberglass boats usually have fiberglass bulkheads. They're hard and very thin. With a rigid boat they form a waterproof seal unless they blow out because you left your boat in the sun and your super-hatch covers were on too tight (and you hadn't drilled those pin holes). In polypropylene boats, the bulkheads are usually thick (1-1/2" to 2") and soft. They flex with the boat and usually leak a little water, though I've received reports that some of the newer boats may not. For Florida, it probably doesn't matter what type you get. In fact, two of my boats have no bulkheads and I keep them filled with blown-up flotation bags in the shape of cones that fit very nicely. I replace these with cone-shaped bags used for storage when I camp. As long as the flotation doesn't spring a leak (all the cheap ones do eventually, so bring a patch kit or buy good ones), they work almost as well as bulkheads. I mention this only to help those of you who want to buy good, but cheap, and have found a boat without bulkheads.

5. Doubles/Singles

When I switched from canoes to kayaks, my wife and I had lengthy discussions about whether to buy a double or two single kayaks. For those of you who don't know, a single kayak has one cockpit and a double kayak has two. (They do make a three-holer to include a kid but I've never paddled one.) Because the doubles were more than twice as expensive as the singles, we decided on two singles. This would allow us to develop our individual potentials without performing physical mayhem on each other when things turned bad. It would also allow one person to lift and move a boat by him/her self, giving more flexibility to the type of tripping we could do.

A year or so later, we rented some doubles with our teenage sons and couldn't believe what a pain in the rear end they were (the boats). We were forever banging paddles into each other as our cadences faltered, turning in the wrong directions because "left" and "right" always seemed to get screwed up, and generally realizing that we needed a choreographer to get through it all successfully. It didn't take long for us to conclude that you needed a lot of practice with your partner and had to have a great sense of humor.

We later learned that the person who rented us the boats forgot to give us the rudders that went with them. Paddling the same boats with rudders two years later in Glacier Bay changed my mind dramatically about doubles. In fact, we bought one a few years ago and love it. Never, never, get a double without a rudder unless your pairbonding is very stable and strong. Recently a company has started producing an 18' convertible composite boat with a large front hatch that can be fitted with a seat to make a double from a single. I've not had a chance to paddle this boat, and have some questions about how it would sit in the water under various conditions, but it might be worth a look if you can't make up your mind about what you should buy.

Here are some advantages and disadvantages of:

Singles:
1. Cheaper
2. Lighter to cartop and portage
3. Go on your own (a no-no in serious sea kayaking)
4. Go at your own pace
5. Stop where you want

Doubles:
1. Take a friend and/or dog
2. Stores more gear
3. Larger size is more stable
4. Faster than a single
5. Less energy to paddle
6. More easily sailable

Illustration # 1-6. Double Kayak

Every family should have at least one double and two singles. That way you can outfit your own expeditions. (See Illustration # 1-6. Double Kayak.)

6. Sails/Parasails/Kites

On those hard days of paddling when the wind shifts from your face to your back (seemingly a very rare occurrence), your mind will search out ways to use some form of sail to help the boat along with less effort. Everything from stretching a rain jacket over a paddle to kites and full double sails, lee boards and outriggers have been tried. All are effective to one degree or another. I've tried all but the outriggers. Here are my personal observations.

For Florida, none will be totally satisfactory. The winds are rarely consistent enough and the coasts have so many sinuosities that voyages rarely continue in a straight line long enough to allow all but the most elaborate and complete sailing rigs to work for very long. The reason for this is that kayaks can only sail against the wind (tack) with some form of leeboard that descends far down into the water to keep the wind from blowing the boat sideways. Boats without these leeboards can only sail downwind. The simpler the rig, the less "off" the wind you can sail.

Kites and parasails will give you about 15 degrees on either side of the direction of the wind. Most shoreline paddles, at least on the Gulf Coast, will change as much as 15 to 90 degrees during any two-hour paddle. The wind may also shift during this time. The other problem with kites and parasails is launching them. I was never successful launching one from the boat while moving. I tried a few times and found that the boat was moving with the air and I couldn't get enough lift. It might have worked better in harder winds (18 knots up). I've started kites from shore and got into the boat while the kite was soaring and had a wonderful half hour. I've read about inflatable kites that are easy to launch but have never seen one. My experience in Florida is that if you have a parasail or kite, they're fun to have along, but you won't use them much unless you do a lot of open water crossings. However, when things work, it's quite pleasant to be pulled along for a while by that brightly colored kite in the sky.

The really elaborate sailing rigs are based on sailboard designs and do a great job. Unfortunately, they add 15 to 20 pounds and take up a fair amount of space (a tube 8″ in diameter and 4′ long) when not in use. They also require a new type of balance to accommodate wind shifts. I own one of these rigs and have enjoyed it a lot the three or four times I've used it over the last few years. These rigs are usually designed for very fat, stable singles or double kayaks only. They just aren't stable enough for the normal single kayak unless you have unusual balance and courage. A few specialty manufacturers offer outriggers for kayak sailing rigs that will make the boat much more stable. Unfortunately, that doesn't solve the problems raised below.

There are two problems with these sailing rigs. The biggest one is that you have to decide if you're a sailor or a kayaker. That may sound like a small problem, but mindset often seems to control what I do. I don't consider myself a sailor so I usually don't even think about bringing the sail. Which brings up the second problem, deciding whether to spend the energy to load the sail and set it up. Once again, not a big problem. But it's crazy how often I decide to take the sail and then leave it at the last minute because "it's not worth the effort." Since I get much of my exercise from paddling, it's hard to make the transition. I guess I'll break through this year and take it on my annual Gulf excursion, which may change my perspective. Or maybe I'll plan a sailing expedition and not worry about paddling.

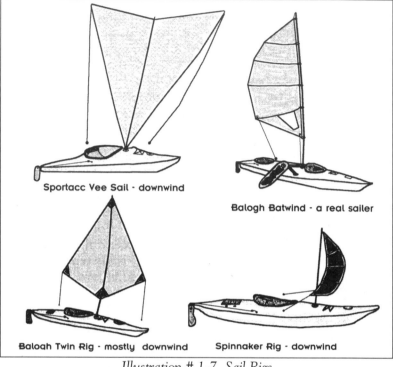

Illustration # 1-7. Sail Rigs

The other available sail rigs include a variety of downwind masted units that are a step above rain gear attached to the paddle. They can be more effective, depending on the size. I've made two different kinds using various types of plastic and aluminum pipe and ripstop nylon sails. Commercial units are available. They move you along at just about the same speed you would make if you were paddling under the same conditions. Nice for a rest, but it doesn't seem to last long. (See Illustration # 1-7. Sail Rigs.)

7. Collapsibles

A number of different kayaks can be taken apart for transportation or storage. The traditional models were the Folboats and Kleppers that were made of rubberized material stretched over ribs. The new kinds include inflatable plastic rafts shaped like kayaks and fiberglass boats that are cut in three pieces at the bulkheads and bolted back together for use.

The modern canvas-covered boats have been used extensively since the late 1800s with good results. Today, I doubt you'd want one with all the other choices available unless you needed the collapsible feature to transport it by air or public transportation in foreign lands. For Florida, it's probably better to rent a rigid boat when you get here. Except for a few new ones on the market, most singles weigh in the 85-pound range and doubles well over 100 pounds. In addition, they take from 1/2 hour to 4 hours to set up (depending on what model and how much you've practiced). The costs are also steeper than most of the plastic or glass boats. They start in the $1,200s and may go over $4,000. They don't like oyster bars one bit and can abrade on sandy shores. I've never paddled one so I can't describe how they feel, but most information is that if you can get over the other drawbacks they do fine.

The inflatable kayaks (often called "rubber duckies") seem to be limited to river play and a few hardy souls who try to use them in the ocean (Audrey Southerland paddled over 4,000 miles around Alaska in one but would rather have used a lightweight fiberglass if she could have found one). They really aren't sea kayaks. They seem a little flimsy to me, though I've never paddled one.

The newest gimmick is the three-piece glass boat that can be disassembled for travel. I say "gimmick" because they make me a little nervous. Each piece is bulkheaded and the bulkheads are bolted together to assemble. There isn't any reason it can't work, but all those holes feel more like a colander than a sea kayak. If you need a boat that comes apart, this may be what you're looking for. In fact, I've seen advertisements for companies that will cut up your existing boat and a *Sea Kayaker* magazine article about a do-it-yourself approach. I'd talk to someone who paddles one of these before I'd buy one or cut up mine.

Summary

As a first boat, buy the cheapest you can find that's at least 14' long, has a useable rudder, a comfortable cockpit and seat, and hatches that are big enough for your gear. Except for unusual luck, a used "Tupperware" boat is your best bet. Save the other boats for your No. 2.

Chapter 2
PADDLES

You may think this is a simple subject that doesn't warrant a chapter's worth of writing. You're wrong. When kayakers talk, it's about boats and paddles, usually in equal amounts. While the boat is what keeps you afloat, the paddle is what makes you go. I just finished reading a seven-page essay on the "Quest for the Perfect Paddle," by Matt Broze in *Sea Kayaker* magazine (Vol. 8, #4, Spring 1992, p. 39). It's one of a long line of articles written about paddles in various publications by various aficionados in the kayaking world. It's a great essay with all kinds of technical jargon that everyone should read in deciding on their perfect paddle. Unfortunately, once you read it, you probably won't be much closer than when you started. It's not the fault of the article, it's the fault of humans of different sizes, boats of different sizes and different paddling conditions and objectives.

There is no perfect paddle either generically or just for you. The only thing that I feel comfortable saying about paddles is that the cheap, heavy clunkers will kill you if you do more than a few miles and the super-expensive, high-tech featherweights will be wasted on most kayakers. Between those ranges, 98% of you will be more than satisfied.

In broad terms, you need a paddle that won't break and will propel you through the water at a reasonable rate of speed when you want it to, without making you think about attaching a motor.

The variations available are mind-boggling. They include all kinds of materials, shapes sizes, and even colors. Some break apart into two pieces (intentionally) and some are one piece, feathered or straight.

For those of you who don't know what "feathering" is, it means having the blades of the paddle turned at an angle to each other. (See Illustration # 2-1. Feathered and Unfeathered Paddles.) The ongoing debate on whether to use paddles straight or feathered will be covered in detail in Chapter 5, "Techniques." Everyone seems to have an opinion about this but mine makes the most sense.

Like boats, paddles are very personal. Try them out and find one you like and can afford.

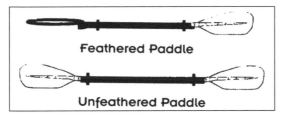

Illustration # 2.1. Feathered and Unfeathered Paddles

1. Materials

Paddles are usually made of wood, fiberglass, or aluminum/plastic combinations. The high-tech fiberglass paddles may include Kevlar and graphite strips to lighten and strengthen. Wood requires the most maintenance (oiling or revarnishing) but has the greatest beauty. Break-apart wooden paddles usually use some form of brass fittings to connect the pieces together.

The aluminum/plastic models have aluminum shafts with plastic blades. The shafts bend and the blades break more easily (possibly because they are treated more shabbily, being cheaper). Many of the break-apart models can be fitted with individual handles and used as canoe paddles when not kayaking.

I've used all three types and find that I prefer fiberglass for reasons that are listed in the other sections.

2. Length

Kayak paddles can be purchased from 80″ to 120″ long. The one you need depends on your size, the boat size and the type of paddling you do. I traded for a paddle once that was a lot smaller than I expected (90″). I loved it. It felt light and fast. After a week or so, I started having shoulder problems. I went back to my longer paddle (108″) and the shoulder got better. I'm sure there's a good explanation. I now use a paddle between 98″ and 108″ for different purposes. The shorter paddle is my deepwater or river paddle. My longer paddle is my shallow-water coastal paddle. I've used them in each situation without much trouble; it's just that when you can afford two, you might as well use them.

There are a number of formulas used by various people to determine proper paddle length. I've tried to use them all at one time or another. I won't give you any here because they're mostly geared to very specific circumstances that don't often happen in the present real world. I wonder what size paddles the Greenland Eskimos would have used if they had fiberglass. I'm sure you'll run into someone who has memorized all the proper trendy formulas who'll be happy to share his "knowledge" with you when you buy your first paddle.

The reason I use the longer paddle on the coast is that the part of the Gulf of Mexico where I usually paddle is very shallow. I've paddled for five or six hours in water that averaged 9″ to 10″ deep. A long paddle with a blade shape that's compatible will allow most of the blade to be under water at the proper time for maximum propulsion under these conditions. Short paddles can't reach out far enough. Paddling under these conditions is not fun. However, it's less "not fun" when you have the right paddle.

Most smaller people (I'm 5′10″ and consider myself average) feel more comfortable with smaller paddles. I don't know if that's because of the weight or the feel of the stroke. Larger people seem to like longer paddles. No matter what anyone tells you, you'll probably like any good paddle you get used to that doesn't cause physical problems.

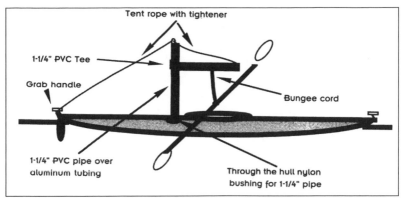

Tent rope with tightener

1-1/4" PVC Tee

Grab handle

Bungee cord

1-1/4" PVC pipe over
aluminum tubing

Through the hull nylon
bushing for 1-1/4" pipe

Illustration # 2-2. Paddle Suspension Rig

3. Weight

The lighter the paddle, the better it is—as long as it meets the
other parameters in this chapter. However, weight is only really
important once it reaches a certain pound range. Any paddle that
weighs more than 2 pounds is getting a little heavy. Just remember the million times you have to lift and stroke with it. I guess it's
just like hiking boots. Every extra pound on your feet is like ten in
your pack (that sounds stupid but really does seem to work out).
The pros talk about the weight of the blade being more important
than the weight of the shaft. Something to do with fulcrums and
swinging weights at the end of a rope, but it didn't make much
sense to me. Holding up the total weight seemed more important.
In fact, I built a rig for my wife that would allow the paddle to be
suspended in front of her on a bungee cord from a bar over her
head in order to relieve some of the weight. It seemed to work.
Reports in one of the magazines claimed this would relieve 40% of
the paddling effort (see Illustration # 2-2. Paddle Suspension Rig
and Appendix 2 for construction instructions).

4. Shape

Within limits, the shape of the paddle blade is of real importance.
Shapes range from the modern synthetic blade that looks like a
twisted spoon or futuristic wing to the wooden Greenland-style

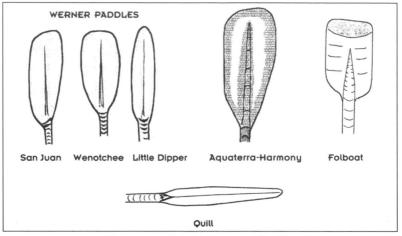

Illustration # 2-3. Types of Paddles

long, narrow blade. Each type has benefits and drawbacks. (See Illustration # 2-3. Types of Paddles.)

The first paddle I used was a wooden Klepper paddle with a brass-covered blunt tip. I liked it. It worked well but it was a little heavy. Besides, it wasn't mine. The next one I used was a full-bladed fiberglass spoon-shaped (Aquaterra/Harmony) paddle that was a lot lighter than the wooden one, was elliptical in the grip area and a lot more comfortable. I also tried a very expensive graphite model that was the same shape but even lighter. I didn't like the graphite as well (nor the additional $100). About that same time, I read about the Greenland paddles that were supposed to be easier to stroke. I tried one called a "quill" and bought it. For the next year I paddled with my quill, extolling its virtues to all who would listen. It was wood and a little heavier than the Aquaterra/Harmony, but it was markedly easier to move through the water. My only problem was that I always finished last whenever a group of us went paddling. In order to keep up I had to increase my stroke to a level that was not very comfortable. When my paddling friends started complaining about slowing down to talk to me, I decided to try something else. I bought a Werner San Juan. This has been my main paddle for six years. It doesn't paddle much differently from the Aquaterra/Harmony for speed/effort, but the long shaft and somewhat narrower blade has worked the best in the shallow water I usually paddle. I own two of them.

Whitewater racers have used a molded paddle blade that's designed on a computer and shaped like a wing with a bent shaft. For a long time, sea kayakers have avoided it because it didn't feel right for the price. More recently this has begun to change. They're supposed to be more efficient and faster. I've never used one so I can't offer any advice.

5. Price

Unless mass production catches up with the kayaking business, paddles (and practically everything else with "kayak" attached to it) will be expensive. Expect to spend $135 to $250 for a good paddle. The best of the bent winged paddles of graphite can go for more than $450. You can buy the clunkers for $30 to $65, but if you can afford it, start with a good paddle. One writer has suggested, however, that if you buy the clunker to start with, you can always use it as your backup when you get a better one. You will also really appreciate a good paddle after using a clunker for a while. Breakdown paddles are usually a little bit more expensive but worth the difference if you travel in a car.

Illustration # 2-4. Drip Ring

6. Drip Rings

Drip rings are rubber or plastic circles that are placed around the paddle shaft, between your hands and the blades, to catch the water drips that run off the blades as you paddle. (See Illustration # 2-4. Drip Ring.) They should be placed far enough away from your hands so that the drips will end up outside the cockpit and not run down your hands or onto your lap. For new paddlers, it hardly seems to matter. Water always seems to end up in the cockpit if you're not wearing a skirt when you first start paddling. There would be a lot more water without drip rings. They are a marvelous invention for which someone ought to have been awarded a Nobel prize for design. Never leave home without your drip rings firmly attached.

7. Take-Apart Paddles

I've found that paddles that are made to break apart are a lot more convenient than those that don't, for two reasons. First, sea kayak paddles tend to be longer than whitewater paddles. Getting an 8" paddle into a 4' car trunk can be a problem. Second, a take-apart paddle will give you the option to feather your paddle when the need strikes. Some of the newer paddles will let you feather by degrees to get the exact angle that works for you though this added complexity just confuses me. The only downside is the inherent weakness that may exist at the joint. I've never had a problem with this under the paddling conditions I've experienced, nor have I read of any problems with the newer paddles. If you have a choice, get a take-apart paddle.

Summary

Buy a paddle that works for you. Try a few. Be willing to spend more than you think you should. After you buy your second or third, you'll begin to reach a reasonable level of satisfaction.

Chapter 3

GENERAL GOODIES AND SAFETY STUFF

1. Skirts

The most important piece of safety equipment on your boat will be your spray skirt. If you don't have a skirt, don't paddle your boat in anything but flat and warm ocean water in a location near shore where it can be easily emptied. The skirt is that strange-looking thing that connects to the coaming of the cockpit and extends in a tube up your body to your armpits. (See Illustration # 3-1. Spray Skirt.) It should seal the boat off from any water entering as a result of wave action, rain, paddle drips, or stupid dumps. Not only is it good for water protection, it's also good for the cold. Since it seals off the interior of the boat, it traps nice warm air where you need it in the winter and allows you surprising comfort in cold weather. Unfortunately, it does the same thing in hot weather as well. More on that later.

The earliest Eskimo skirts were sealskin hooded pull-over jackets that fit tightly around the wrists and face and attached to the cockpit. They totally enclosed the body of the wearer and sealed it into the boat. The modern skirt attaches to the boat and is suspended from the wearer by suspenders that keep the top of the skirt high off the boat deck.

Modern skirts are usually made from two different materials or a hybrid. The most useful for Florida is the lightweight, coated,

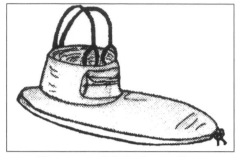

Illustration # 3-1. Spray Skirt

nylon skirt with suspenders. It's also the cheapest. This skirt is not good for surf or heavy wave action. It is, however, relatively cool, and can be worn through most of what you will face in Florida waters. I've used my nylon skirt in heavy surf with reasonable results, but I wouldn't recommend it or make a practice of it.

The most effective skirt in keeping water out (and in) is one made from neoprene rubber. It seals better at the cockpit and on your body. It's horrible for Florida except during dead winter because it's so hot. These skirts are made for cold, whitewater streams and should be used there. The danger of these skirts in Florida is that they are so uncomfortable under most conditions that you might be tempted to leave yours at home or use it and die from hyperthermia (heat stroke).

The hybrid skirt is made of a neoprene bottom and a nylon top. The neoprene bottom seals the cockpit and maintains a strong platform across the cockpit to keep crashing waves from caving in the skirt. The nylon top can be opened and will allow air to circulate and keep you cool. It also contains a nice pocket for things you want nearby. These are probably the best all around but are the most expensive ($95+). They are still hotter than I like, though we have two of them and use them when touring with our double.

A few manufacturers have come out with skirts specifically for warm water paddlers. The one I saw in a catalogue looked like half cockpit cover that runs from the front of the cockpit to your body with a small flange that turns up. I presume this flange is there to deflect water rolling over your bow. It is certainly better than no skirt in rough weather but I have doubts whether it can do much more than keep out occasional spray.

Putting on a skirt can be difficult, particularly if it's wet and muddy and you're doing it while sitting in the boat as a thunderstorm approaches. Try to remember to put your skirt on before you put on your personal flotation device (PFD) or rain gear. We paddled for three days as 12″ of rain fell without getting wet inside the boat because of good rain gear and reasonably tight skirts (no sexist comments are permitted by kayakers about skirts — we leave that to the rednecks). Rain jackets go on the *outside* of the skirt so the water runs off the skirt and boat and not into the boat and onto your nice dry clothes. Remember the order: paddling clothes, skirt, rain gear, and then PFD.

2. Personal Flotation Devices (PFDs)

PFDs are the second most important pieces of safety equipment. The only reason I don't consider them as important as a skirt is that you can paddle safely without a PFD in rough water unless you go over and out. You can't paddle safely in rough water without a skirt. Once the waves fill up your cockpit, you're dead meat. However, let me say this loud and clear: Always wear your PFD when paddling your boat.

Now that I've said that, I can tell you what I do and why. Don't even think about doing this unless you take full responsibility for your reckless behavior as I do. I always carry a good PFD with me, though I rarely wear it in Florida. In fact, I have only worn my wonderful bright-red PFD in three circumstances. First is going through surf. The possibility of being knocked out of your boat and becoming injured or disoriented in the surf is higher than in any other circumstance you'll meet in Florida. Particularly if it's big East Coast surf during winter storms or hurricanes (don't be out in these). The second is in high winds and rough seas that sometimes show up during bay crossings. This has happened to me once or twice in nine years, so don't worry too much about it. The third circumstance is when it's cold and I forget to bring my warm jacket.

When I'm not wearing my PFD, it's always within easy reach, either behind my seat (giving the seat back a little support) or under a nearby bungee cord on deck. Florida does require that you have some form of Coast Guard-approved flotation device in most boats.

There are a number of types and styles of PFDs. The best ones are usually expensive and should last as long as your boat if you take care of them. The front zip type with plastic zippers and a waist belt with soft flexible foam seem to be the best. It's important to have a short PFD so it will sit on top of the skirt. When you sit in a boat, the most comfortable PFDs should come from your shoulders to the top of the cockpit, not to your waist. A longer PFD gets pushed up over your head if you're wearing a skirt (as I said above, if it's important to wear a PFD, it's more important to wear a skirt). The shorter the PFD, the more comfortable. It will also help if the foam rubber in the PFD goes over the shoulders. This will allow you to carry your boat over your shoulder without the cockpit digging into your collarbone.

In the last five or six years, lightweight, flat PFDs have come on the market that look really cool. I haven't wanted to spend the money so I haven't had a chance to try one out, but they look great and seem to solve a lot of problems with the earlier models. These have been developed specifically for kayaks and come with lots of belts and buckles, neat pockets, and super colors. Because they eliminate or reduce the amount of foam on the backs they are more comfortable to use with kayak seat backs and those with mesh backs are a lot cooler. They're very expensive but seem to be very useful in our warmer climate.

Florida law no longer allows boat cushions as approved flotation devices. You must have wearable approved PFDs of some form. The old-style flotation collars will work, but are harder to get on and look very "unkayaky." Pay for a good PFD and take care of it. It may save your life some day.

3. Sponges/Pumps

Sponges are very important equipment for kayaks. Since most kayaks have no way of draining water out without being turned upside down, and even then leave a cupful or two of water, a simple bailing method is required. Sponges generally do the job. Sponges come in all sizes, shapes, and colors. Buy a large one at your local supermarket. When it falls apart, buy another one. It's amazing how much water you can track into the boat by getting in and out or just sloppy paddling. They're also good to keep things clean. If your boat goes over, the sponge will eventually bail it out (in time). Usually you'll just stand up in the shallow water and turn it over or drag it to the closest land. Then use the sponge to get the rest.

Pumps are a lot faster in bailing a boat than a sponge. Unfortunately, they do little for that last cup or two of water and nothing for keeping the boat clean. Some of the more expensive boats have built-in pumps just behind the seat. High-volume hand pumps are available in the $20 to $30 range and should be equipped with a flotation collar so they don't sink when they fall overboard. They do a good job. Electric pumps are available, but I've never met anyone who ever used one.

I bought a nice pump with a flotation collar after being without one for five years. I've used it once to pump out a partially filled boat and it worked very well. It also worked for water fights. The reason pumps are important in cold water is to get the water out as fast as possible to avoid hypothermia. Since the coldest water you will find in Florida is the warmest you could ever expect in the Northwest, it isn't as much of a problem here. We could have sponged out the boat in five minutes and it took us about one minute to pump it.

4. Hypothermia/Throws/Paddle Floats/Sea Socks

After drowning, hypothermia is the most dangerous condition you can experience in a sea kayak outing. It means your body core temperature has dropped below what your body energy sources can maintain. It can be fatal if not treated rapidly. There are whole books and a lot of sections of other books about outdoor activities on the subject. Read up on it. Take it seriously. You can get hypothermia in water less than 85 degrees and air temperatures in the 70s, though it would take quite a while in both cases. Windy, wet weather can cause it even under relatively mild conditions if you're out long enough with improper clothing and food. You would be less likely to suffer hypothermia in Florida than in the cold north, but underdressed, unprepared paddlers can become hypothermic anywhere. How to avoid hypothermia? Dress properly or carry additional clothing layers. Know your susceptibility to cold.

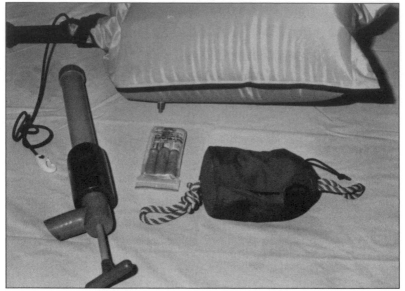

Illustration # 3-2. Safety Equipment

Hyperthermia (heat stroke) can be a problem for anyone who goes outside in the summer in Florida. For kayakers, it shouldn't be much of one if you're careful and pour water over your head from time to time.

Throw ropes and paddle floats are pieces of safety equipment nice to have but rarely used. (See Illustration # 3-2. Safety Equipment.) I own both and have used neither. Throw ropes are lengths of heavy duty floating rope stuffed into a bag that also floats. In a rescue attempt, the end of the rope is held and the bag thrown, allowing the rope to feed out because of the force of the throw. The person to whom the bag is thrown can grab onto a loop of the rope that has been drawn through and sewn to the bag.

A paddle float is a bag of coated nylon that you blow up and slip over the blade of the paddle where it is securely fastened. The purpose of the float is to establish a non-sinking platform in the water on one end of the paddle so it will act as an outrigger, giving stability and support for reentry or just to keep the boat upright in heavy seas. It's a pretty good self rescue device.

Sea socks are waterproof coated nylon bags that fit inside the kayak and attach to the cockpit coaming. The paddler sits inside the sock. Its purpose is to provide a limited area for water to get into if the boat goes over. It was developed mainly for boats without bulkheads or rudders since you wouldn't need one with good bulkheads and you'd abrade it to unusability with a rudder. If the boat does go over, you can try to empty the water by pulling out the sock or bail it. I tried one once and didn't like it.

5. Compass/Flares/Noisemakers

Every kayaker needs a compass. Having paddled in fog without being able to see shore, I can attest to the need for a compass even for coastal paddling in Florida. The only question is whether you need one of those neat ones that affix to your boat, a cheap one you carry in your map case (or on a string around your neck), or a fancy GPS unit. I have an easy answer. Buy the cheap one. Here's why.

The first boat I took on an expedition around a portion of the Gulf had a beautiful compass about 5″ in diameter built into the deck of the boat just in front of the cockpit. It was big enough to be easily readable from the seat and worked great on training runs. It cost over $150. From the first day of the camping trip, the readings made no sense (the sun does not rise in the north in Florida). Since I didn't need a compass on that trip, I didn't worry about it. About halfway through, I tried an experiment. I moved my camera bag from between my legs directly under the compass. You're right. The compass started to work properly. I solved the problem but I didn't have any other place to store the camera, so I put it back.

Since that time I've used a cheap plastic Silva compass and never had another problem. These small hand-held compasses can be placed on top of a map for better direction location and can be stored in the map case. When I have to steer by compass, I stick it under the bungee in front of me. It's worked well so far. Unless the dealer is willing to throw it in free with the boat, I wouldn't spend the money on a built-in. I'll spend more time on the GPS below, but suffice it to say these wonderful devices need batteries, and if you don't have them when you need them you might as well use the GPS for a fishing weight.

Flares—those things you shoot off into the air or hold in your hand—emit a bright light to help people find you. I always carry a

set with me even for day paddles. I've never used one. I'm not even
sure the ones I have still work. They're in a small package that cost
about $25 and doesn't take up much room. Why not take them along?

Florida boating law requires boats of a certain size to have
some form of noisemaker to warn off other boaters.. I keep a plastic whistle in my deck box. They're nice to have to signal to fel-
low paddlers if you're in trouble or just want their attention. You
can also buy obnoxious little compressed air horns. We bought
some before we went paddling in Alaska to scare off bears. We did-
n't use them for that purpose but they sure scared the hell out of
us when they went off accidentally in the luggage.

6. Binoculars

Binoculars are not essential but are a good piece of equipment to
have along with you. A medium- to low-priced pair ($90 dis-
counted) of small roof prisms that are rubber-coated and water-
resistant will do. Anywhere from 7 to 10 power is usable. You'll
want something that you can put out of the way, can stand a little
splashing of saltwater and will not be knocked out of alignment by
rough handling. I'm a birder so I always have a pair handy.
However, they can be very important for sighting landmarks, paddling companions, and stopping places from the low vantage point
of a sea kayak. They may save you a lot of paddling time.

I can remember paddling out of my way toward a little island
that got up and moved away as I got close. (It's amazing how ducks
in large rafts can move.) If I had taken my binoculars out, this
wouldn't have happened. (It still would have moved away but I
wouldn't have paddled toward it!) Because of the low relief on
Florida's coast, it's often hard to spot river mouths, channels entrances and exposed oyster bars from a distance. It's nice to know
where you're going when muscle power is the only way you'll get
there and direction mistakes can cost a lot of lost time and effort.

I use a pair of Minolta Pocket 10x25 6.5 degree wide-angle,
multi-coated that cost around $120 discounted ($150 retail). They
fit in my shirt pocket and weigh about one pound. There are a lot
of good binoculars in this range.

7. GPS Systems

A GPS system does the same thing using satellite broadcasts timed by atomic clocks. GPS is accurate within 3 meters of any spot on earth. I originally thought these units were expensive toys until I got one for my birthday a few years ago and had a chance to use it on a trip in the Everglades and Ten Thousand Islands. I've changed my mind completely. These things are so much fun!! There were GPS units in three of the boats, each being operated at different levels of sophistication and expertise. The most learned of us had looked at a map and pre-entered the coordinates of each change in direction as well as the location of points of interest. The second most experienced user had entered the points of interest and the least experienced (yours truly) knew enough to turn the unit on and page through the various screens but had pre-entered nothing.

After paddling across a wide bay, we entered the mangrove islands and I was immediately lost. I pressed the key that let me enter the present location into the GPS but had no idea where to go. At that point the learned one pointed to a narrow gap between islands and the other agreed, based on his knowledge of our ultimate destination. We continued like this for the next six hours until we got to our camp site. It might have been fun paddling around in circles and getting lost for the night with all the mosquitoes, but I guess I'm getting too old or sensible for that and was quite satisfied to know where I was and where I was going.

I learned a lot about the value of GPS on that trip. I entered the turn points at each location and was able to find my way back with no problems. I was also able to use the GPS as a compass, speedometer, clock, and direction finder. With the waypoint system engaged, I was able to estimate time of arrival at each turn point as well as check distances. It was more information than I needed, and I don't use it on every trip, but it sure was fun to have that knowledge and the safety it provided. Acceptable GPS systems can be purchased from $100 on up depending on the features you want and I would suggest it for anyone paddling Florida's low relief coast line.

8. Cell Phones

In the earlier version of this book, I was amazed at how a sinking motorboater used a cell phone to direct the Coast Guard to his location and save him from drowning off Miami. I predicted then that as coverage increased, cell phones would become a part of paddling safety gear. Well, it's almost come true. For most areas of the state there is coverage well off shore. However, and that's a big however, coverage is not complete in many of the best paddling areas and may never reach those spots until we shift from towers to satellites (except for those who have expensive satellite phones and service). In addition, that little man who goes around and tests where coverage is available rarely does so in a boat, so if you want to rely on your cell phone, check with local boaters before you depart to find the coverage in the area you intend to paddle.

9. Miscellaneous

Three pieces of gear that every gadget-head needs to think about are a hand-held marine radio, walkie-talkies and an EPIRB (Emergency Positioning Indicating Radio Beacon). The hand-held marine radios range in cost from $150 to $500. They do all kinds of neat things with buttons and dials and are useful for finding out weather forecasts, communicating with passing freighters and monitoring fish stories from the locals. They are also nice to have to keep in touch with paddlers who separate or who go to shore looking for good camping spots. I lusted after a pair since I ordered my first Dick Tracy radio 50 years ago (which didn't work) and finally got them. Once or twice they were useful, but I've never learned their battery life and am afraid to turn them on except for weather reports so I'll have fresh batteries if an "emergency" arises. I'm not very logical about this sort of thing. These radios transmit on line of sight from the top of your antenna to the top of the receiving station. That's around 3 miles kayak to kayak and probably 10 to 20 or so to a local Coast Guard station. If you expect to cross the shipping lanes or busy boat channels, they can come in handy.

In the last ten years, two-way communication by walkie-talkie has become very cheap and relatively reliable. If your only need is for short range boat to boat communication, these work well until they get wet. Keep yours in a plastic bag (or spend more and get the waterproof variety) and have fun.

EPIRBs (and other forms of locators) are radio transmitters that, once activated, will allow a satellite going overhead to know where you are and beam this information to rescue people. They come in various types and powers. Having one could prove useful in an emergency, but probably not in Florida. If you just have to own one or the other, a hand-held radio is better in Florida because there is usually someone listening in who can get to you faster. I don't know a kayaker in the Southeast who owns an EPIRB.

Summary

Buy a cheap skirt, an expensive paddle and PFD, then accumulate the rest as you go, unless you are required to do otherwise by the latest boating laws. A sponge, whistle, compass, flares, and binoculars are good to have along. A reliable GPS system is always nice to have if you can afford it, and a cell phone with coverage can be handy. However, much of the rest of the electronic gear, like marine radios, are always fun for the real techhead, but they don't get much use in Florida paddling.

Chapter 4

CLOTHES

The secret of comfortable sea kayak clothing is the same as for most other outdoor activities: "layer," "wick away," and "quick dry." Wear clothes you can take off and put on as the temperatures and conditions change. In Florida, during certain times of the year, you can expect temperatures in the low 30s during the morning and the 80s during the day. One size does not fit all, nor do temperatures change from hot to cold instantly.

Because a kayak cockpit can be closed off by the skirt, it traps the heat from your body, but this is somewhat moderated by the temperature of the water. Since the water temperature rarely gets below the mid-50s, and is often in the 70s fairly late in the year, your below-the-waist clothing may have to be cooler than you expect. You can, of course, vent your cockpit by removing or opening part of your skirt, a move that's not always possible under all situations.

Except under very cold conditions, I paddle in shorts and a long-sleeved shirt for sun and bug protection. I've recently started wearing tights under the shorts for the same reasons. When the temperature drops into the 30s, I put on long pants for warmth. The following describes some of the clothes and materials you may want to consider.

1. Pile/Others

Because of the conditions you'll face in a sea kayak, special clothes may be needed. Actually, you can wear whatever you want, but you may not be able to do it comfortably. The problems are water, heat, cold, and sun. You will almost certainly get wet when you paddle a kayak. Whether this means wet feet or a complete dunking depends on your conditions and skill level. I've found special launching sites in the winter that allowed me to enter the boat from land, put on a skirt and paddle away and return totally dry. It is possible but takes a fair amount of practice and good luck. With Florida's mild conditions, getting a little wet is hardly a problem, but the right clothes can make things a lot more comfortable.

Traditional materials such as cotton and, to a lesser extent, wool hold water and take a long time to dry out. Wet cotton gives you no warmth when wet, where wool retains about 50 to 70% of its original heat-holding ability. Unfortunately, wool is usually heavy and smelly when wet. If it were only a choice between these two materials, wool would be the best bet if you were worried about being cold and cotton if you were concerned about being hot. Fortunately, if your budget permits, high-tech materials are available that will give you a much greater range of comfort and safety.

The paddler's savior is "pile"— a fluffy, synthetic material that has become the standard for cool- and cold-weather outdoor wear. Pile sweaters, pile pants, pile vests, and even pile hats. I took a six-day trip around the Gulf of Mexico in 1985 during early December. The temperatures ranged from 30 to 70 degrees on any one day. I wore a pile sweater every day, and with a little help on cold days, was totally comfortable. When the trip was over, I looked down at my elbows and discovered a series of white lines that were somewhat of a mystery until I rubbed and tasted one. Salt. They were the lines of wet elbows from paddling. I didn't know my elbows got wet — being a perfect paddler, who would have thought I put my elbows in the water? They never felt cold or clammy and the sweater was perfectly dry. It was only when my expedition mates threw me in the water that I realized its real value. When I got out, the water was flowing down my arms. I took the sweater off, centrifuged it around my head a few times, and put it back on. It was still warm and comfortable!

Another advantage of the pile sweater is that it's comfortable in the upper 60s and, with a wind shell, can be comfortable down into the 20s. It has an open weave that lets in the breeze and traps warm air when covered.

Polypropylene, Capolene and other long underwear shirts make good paddling shirts for warm weather. They will protect you from the sun and bugs while still being fairly cool. The lightweight white Capolene is particularly good for summer in Florida though it may not offer enough sun protection for some. If this is the case, shift to midweight.

2. Wet/Drysuits

For the uninitiated, a wetsuit is made from neoprene rubber and works on the principle that the water absorbed into the spongy rubber is heated by your body and is maintained there to keep you warm. A drysuit is made of coated nylon (or non-absorbent rubberized material) with soft rubber closures at the hands, feet and neck. You must wear some form of clothing (usually pile) under it and it should keep you dry and warm. Wetsuits are cheaper and drysuits keep you warmer.

I own a wetsuit. I use it for scuba diving in cold water. The only time I ever wore one in a kayak was when I took my boat into the surf on the East Coast during a heavy southeaster in February. It was my first surf adventure, and the water and air were in the 50s. I needed that wetsuit. Except for those conditions, I can't think of a time when a wetsuit or drysuit would be useful in Florida.

In the Northwest, one of the prime safety rules is to dress in a wetsuit or drysuit to protect yourself from immersion in the cold water. In Alaska, the average survival time in water temperature in the mid-30s is around 7 minutes. This changes to 4 to 8 hours if the water is in the 60s. When the water's in the mid-80s, you probably have a few days if you can keep eating as you float.

The problem in Florida is not the water temperature but the air temperature. Wearing a wetsuit or drysuit when the air is above 60 degrees could cause hyperthermia (heat stroke) if you had to paddle for more than a few minutes. Besides, you'd wrinkle up like a prune and be downright smelly, as well as very uncool. Unless you plan to paddle heavy surf in the winter, forget about the wet/drysuits.

This is not to say that you can't wear a good pullover white-water paddling jacket that's made of urethane-coated nylon and has neoprene closures at the arms and neck. I bought one of these when I first started paddling and found it was more trouble than it was worth. For the rain, I'd rather use a zip-up raincoat that I can take off and put on easily even if it isn't as dry in really rough water. Putting on or removing any clothing once you're under way (except maybe a hat) is never easy. A tight pullover can be downright frightening.

3. Footwear

Kayak footwear can be very important. I intend to dwell on this because the impact of bad shoes can kill a trip. It's easy to keep your feet in good shape if you understand the conditions you'll meet and dress accordingly.

If you intend to paddle only along the sandy beaches of the East Coast, go barefoot (there are a few rocky places along this 200-mile-plus stretch, so be careful at these sites). If you have to land anywhere else you will need some foot protection. Your No. 1 natural enemy in the water will be oyster shells in all but the tropical Keys area and sea urchins and lots of dead and live sharp coral in the Keys. You don't walk oysters or coral barefoot!! Razor-sharp edges remove the bottoms of your feet and keep going from there. Other types of shells, as well as crabs and sting-rays, may also be a problem in the same areas.

On shore there are a whole lot of things that can cause pain to your feet if you're not careful. Broken glass is probably the most important, along with the ubiquitous sandspur, cactus and various roots and vegetables.

I like being barefoot, so I wear as little as I can and then take whatever I wear off when I get in the boat. With a small foam pad under my feet, I'm warm enough down into the low 40s. When I reach shore, I put my footwear back on, depending on landing conditions.

Almost any kind of footwear can work under selected conditions. My observations in this section are for all-around safety and comfort.

Until the introduction of the better water shoes in the last five years I would have said that the ultimate footwear for Florida is the hard-bottom neoprene wetsuit booty with Velcro closures or zippers. I've tried a lot of different footwear under a lot of conditions and have found none better. Now I'm not so sure. The following are observations on various types of footwear and their advantages and disadvantages.

Rubber boots (Juneau sandals). These upper calf to knee-high waterproof boots are a must in Alaska. The water is cold and the bottom is generally rocky. The shore slope is fairly steep and you can get your boat right up to shore to unload. The temperature inside the boat is usually cool. These conditions rarely occur in Florida. The water is usually warm (or not uncomfortable) so you don't need protection from the painful effects of cold water. The water bottoms are either sandy or muddy (with a few exceptions). On the sandy bottoms you won't need any shoes at all (or any will do) and on muddy bottoms, unless it's shallow mud, rubber boots are killers.

On one trip in the Big Bend area of the Gulf, I paddled with two novice kayakers who had just read a sea kayaking book about the Northwest and Alaska. The author had extolled the virtue and necessity of rubber boots so much that these two men had to have them. They were fine getting into the boat (other than dragging in a lot of dirt), but disaster struck when we came back to shore the first time. We had to drag the boats through mud (a common occurrence on this coast) that was covered with an inch or two of water. When the first one cursed loudly as he stepped into a deep mud pocket that allowed water to run over the boot tops, the second one laughed. He laughed until he stepped into a deeper pocket and water and mud also poured into his. The first one, meanwhile, slowly sank deeper into the mud and when he tried to walk again, the foot in his dry boot came out. He landed with his stocking foot on something strange in the mud which caused him to leap into the air (as much as he could with a boot filled with water), coming down on the mud-stuck boot and firmly planting it under mud and water. We searched around and found the boot and moved to shore, wet boots, hurt foot and all.

Both boot owners washed out their boots in clear water and placed them aside to dry, putting on their camp shoes. The next morning, neither pair of boots was dry and both smelled pretty awful. One put his on anyway and the other went barefoot. The barefoot one cut his foot and put on his camp shoes (which remained wet for the rest of the four-day trip) and the other did the same when the odor of his boots became unbearable.

Running shoes. These make very comfortable paddling shoes and are good protection in the water. Unfortunately, mud just sucks them right off no matter how tight you tie them. I once spent five minutes groping around in the mud just to find a missing shoe. It's amazing how a size 10-1/2 can just disappear within inches of where it came off! If you're only going to be on hard bottom or light mud, your old running shoes make a cheap alternative. The only other disadvantage is the slow drying time.

Water sandals. The River Runner type sandals (rubber bottoms and nylon strapping) is another type of footgear that has possibilities for some conditions. They are comfortable, dry quickly, and are easy to put on and take off. They have two problems that can prove to be serious. First, they give you no side protection. Oysters, sea urchins and other baddies have a way of getting you on the side of the foot when you least expect it. This lack of side protection also allows a great mass of shell material to flow in as you walk. Those little pieces of shell make walking in water very uncomfortable. Second, deep mud is not a friend of this footwear. I broke one of these indestructible sandals in half trying to pull my leg out of deep mud. My sporting goods dealer had never seen anything like it, but the factory wouldn't replace them as defective. That leads me to believe that they don't expect the sandals to last under these conditions. I now use mine for camp shoes with thick polypro socks for bug protection.

Forget about zoris (thongs) except for emergency backup. They'll either fall apart or you'll lose them in the mud the first time around unless you're lucky. I have seen old hippies wear these safely, but they're probably protected by some unnamed shoe god that the rest of us have never had a chance to meet.

Water shoes. These are the newer shoe types that have wetsuit booty type bottoms (both hard and soft) with uppers of vari-

ous types of plastics or rubber that dry quickly. I haven't tried these
but I've paddled with people who used some of the earlier, less
expensive varieties and they kept coming off in the mud as well.
Looking at the variety advertised in the catalogues, I would bet you
could find one that would work for you, but not having tried them,
I have no recommendations here. If they work as advertised, these
could be better than wetsuit booties because of the faster drying
potential. The main thing to look for is bottom and side foot protection, keeping out sand and shell pieces, the ability to stay on in
the mud, and the speed of drying.

Wetsuit booties. These have been my footgear of choice since
I started paddling, and I haven't found a reason to change yet
(because they still are holding up and I'm too cheap to buy new
footware). Mine are above ankle height, have a wraparound velcro
closure in the back and hard bottoms. I can put them on and take
them off without effort under most circumstances. Good wetsuit
booties will give you the following advantages. First, they protect
the bottom and sides of your feet from almost all conditions.
Second, they keep your feet warm, even when wet. Third, they
won't come off in mud if tightened sufficiently with the Velcro (I
had to sew on additional Velcro for this). Fourth, they are easy on
and off. The disadvantages are that they're expensive, keep your
feet wet as you paddle if you don't take them off, and they won't
dry in your lifetime (sometimes leading to obnoxious nail fungus).
I also hate how cold and miserable the wet, sandy booties are when
you first put them on in the morning. A note about zippers. If you
don't use your booties often, make sure you lubricate your zippers
after your last use or you may have to junk them.

None of the above is perfect. I want something that will protect my feet from the cold, not be too hot, be easy to put on and
take off, dry in 30 minutes, and be cheap to purchase (or last a lifetime). Let me know when you find them.

4. Hats

Hats to protect you from the sun are very important in Florida.
Unless you're very unlucky, or paddle a lot at night, 80 percent of
the time you'll be in sunlight. If you don't want your brains fried,

protection is called for. Hats with broad brims, neck protection and ventilation are all good things to have. So is a tie-down strap to keep it from getting blown away. Paddling a kayak with one hand while the other holds down your hat is very difficult for the average paddler.

Being mostly bald with a sensitive brain, I own a lot of hats. One of my favorites, a Seattle Sombrero, was bought in Alaska and made by OR in Seattle. It's made of Gore-Tex with some form of moisture-wicking lining. The brim is wide and folds up with Velcro fasteners when you don't need it or want to emulate the Aussie look. It has a great tie-down system. It's miserable for Florida. It's too hot except in the rain and temperatures under 60 degrees (I loved it in Alaska). A friend just gave me a canvas Tilley of similar design. I really like it. If you can afford the money, it may be the hat for you.

Like most other articles of clothing, different situations will require different hats. I have not found a perfect Florida hat. Here's my idea for one: light weight and color, ventilated to allow free air flow for coolness yet will close down around the ears for warmth. It must be rainproof and quick drying. It must tie down, have a broad brim for sun protection and be able to fold up to reduce wind resistance and improve visibility. When you find one like this at a price I can afford, throw it in with those perfect shoes.

5. Rain Gear

Good rain gear is a must in Florida. Though you can usually avoid rain if you're only going out for a few hours, at some point you will probably get wet if you don't have reasonable rain gear. Any cheap plastic button-up (or snap closure) or brown plastic bag will do for the occasional short trip. However, more expensive, high-tech gear will last longer and be a lot more useful in the long run.

My favorite is a Marmot Mountain Gore-Tex Parka that costs a lot of money ($350). It's guaranteed for life and looks great. It's a little long for kayaking (you might try the shorter bicycle variety), but the breathability of the fabric (sweat goes through, rain stays out), the pit zips (zippers that open to expose sweating armpits), tight wrist closures, swell hood and much, much more make it a great jacket and too expensive for most of you. However, there are good Gore-Tex or other breathable fabric jackets on the market that will do.

My Alaska friends tell me that breathable fabrics don't work in salt water and mist, but that's not my experience. I paddled for 10 days in Alaska in salt water and misty rain and did a whole lot better than those wearing coated nylon. Because the coated nylon didn't breathe, the wearers were often as wet inside as out after heavy paddling and did they ever smell! I, on the other hand, was almost odor-free (a relative term after 10 days without a shower). If you remember to wash your Gore-Tex in fresh water after heavy saltwater exposure, it should be fine.

Coated rain gear will work under most circumstances if you need it only during light paddling or occasional thunderstorms. Buy a cheap, lightweight one at your local camping store and take it with you on most paddles if you don't want to take good stuff.

6. Sunglasses

Sunglasses are a must. The less UV light they let in the better. Wraparounds are good. Neutral grays with polarizers help with water vision. Amber is better for depth perception but screws up your color sense if you're doing any photography. Always use tie downs, either neck straps or collar connectors (with alligator clips). On the back of your neck straps you may want to attach a 1-1/2" to 2" circle of closed cell foam rubber so the glasses will float if they come off. A rafter in Utah showed me that little trick. It's probably not necessary unless you expect to be in surf or rough water, but you never know. I always have trouble with neck straps since they are often attached to too many devices — my hat, sunglasses, and a pair of binoculars. Taking off my sunglasses and quickly using my binoculars to view some wild creature often causes strap conflict that can feel irreconcilable. I've learned to cope. Read a good article on sunglasses before buying.

7. Gloves

I find that gloves are like hats but not quite as important. I've paddled for long periods of time with and without gloves. My latest pair is the most satisfying but isn't totally satisfactory. I use bicycle gloves with the fingertips missing. The palms are lightly padded leather and the backs are quick-drying spandex with velcro closures. They give me enough warmth in winter, protection from blisters for long paddles and some sun protection. They dry relatively rapidly (still not fast enough) and fit nicely in my pocket without too much of a bulge. If the palms were made from some non-slip synthetic that didn't hold water, they would be perfect for most conditions. Since the last leather pair fell apart on the last trip, I think I'll shift to Kevlar. Sailing gloves with half fingers may work better but I doubt it.

Here's some of the gloves I've tried and discarded. The piece of equipment voted most useless by all 10 paddlers on the first Big Bend Gulf trip we took in 1985 was poagies. These are the covers that look like mittens but go over your hands and fold around the paddle so you can still grip it with your bare hands inside. They were designed for whitewater paddling where paddle grip was essential, cold water and cold weather were normal, and no gloves had been developed that would allow firm control. This type of grip isn't necessary with a sea kayak except in surf or rough conditions rarely found in Florida. I was given a pair of neoprene poagies and bought a pair of coated nylon and pile poagies before I did much paddling. I've never worn the neoprene ones (I cut them up for knee pads), and I've used the nylon ones once when the weather was in the 20s and I couldn't find my other gloves. They worked fine, if a little warm. Don't waste money on these.

Neoprene diving gloves work okay but I find them uncomfortable for long paddles where you continue to flex your hands as you paddle. These gloves have a stable shape and you're always pressing against the shape of the glove at some part of your stroke. The few times I wore neoprene gloves, they were too hot and wet inside for me. They also chafed in a few spots. Maybe the newer ones are a little better made. They give a good grip on the paddle but that's not enough to overcome their negatives.

I tried polypropylene gloves (usually advertised as "liners") on two trips, but found they fell apart by the end of the trip and the odor got so bad that I was continuously rinsing them out. Since the only real advantage to polypro was its quick drying (and cheapness), continuous wetting seemed to cancel any advantage it may have had on that score.

For day trips, gloves will rarely be necessary except for cold weather. On longer trips, you need protection from blisters and the sun. Any type of gloves will work for short trips. For long ones, take some care and get gloves that will fit the conditions you expect to meet — and bring along a spare pair.

8. Tights

One new addition to my wardrobe is a pair of long, lycra tights. I found them on sale at a camping/running store and have been in love ever since. They paddle cool (or warm with overpants), keep the sun off without giving you heat prostration and help protect you from small biting critters when you go ashore. They don't dry all that quickly, but your body heat warms them up so fast that the momentary discomfort of putting on yesterday's wet tights eases very rapidly. I sometimes wear a bathing suit over the tights for abrasion resistance and modesty. If a mild rash that developed after my last trip is a result of wearing the same tights four days in a row, I might change my recommendation.

Summary

You can paddle a sea kayak in anything that allows you to move the paddle easily and operate the rudder. However, comfort and safety dictate that you be willing to make some allowances from your standard wardrobe. For the most comfortable and safest clothes for Florida in the winter, try a pile sweater, shorts over tights, Velcro closure wetsuit booties (or your favorite water shoe), Gore-Tex raincoat, Tilley hat, sunglasses and sailing or bicycle cut-off gloves. If you don't want to spend the money, try an old bathing suit, a cotton T-shirt, wool jacket, your oldest running shoes, $3 plastic raincoat with plastic snaps and your adjustable peaked cap that says "Don't f . . . with me cause I'm a real trucker," or something like that. Either wardrobe will work for most conditions.

Chapter 5

TECHNIQUES

I will probably be embarrassed by my mistakes. What I will attempt to do is give some advice about certain phases of the sport I picked up (stole) from other writers and personal experience and relate that to Florida. There are a fair number of good books on sea kayaking that will give you more than you want to know. Try a few of those and take lessons from a good instructor. (See Appendix # 3.)

1. Getting in the Boat and Going

Though each boat is a little different, the entrance techniques are pretty much the same. Find a way to drop your rear end onto the seat as soon as you can without turning the boat over. This puts the center of gravity as low as possible as soon as possible for optimum stability. The heavier the rear end, the greater the stability. Many variations are possible or necessary depending on whether you get in from a dock, beach, or open water. Placing both hands behind you on either side of the rear of the cockpit while performing the above gyrations helps to stabilize the boat.

In Florida, you will probably enter your boat from a beach or gently sloping boat ramp. The easiest way to enter under these circumstances is to place the boat with the front or back just touching bottom with the opposite end floating in deeper water. It

Illustration # 5-1.
Getting In

should be deep enough for the boat to still float even after you enter with only a small part touching the bottom for stability. Once you're in and settled, push off with your hands or (very carefully) with your paddle.

Boats with small cockpits may force you to slide your legs in first while sitting on the back of the cockpit (if it's strong enough) or suspended from hands on the support base (bulkhead area) behind the cockpit. Once the legs get in far enough, drop your rear end onto the seat. Wriggle around and get comfortable.

If the cockpit is large enough (or your legs short enough), straddle the boat just in front of the cockpit, drop your rear end onto the seat and then pull your legs in. This last method will allow you to take off your shoes or shake out mud before you put your feet into the cockpit.

If the above two methods don't work, try the following. Step into the middle of the cockpit in front of the seat with one foot while maintaining your balance with a hand on either side of the back of the cockpit. Bring in the other leg and slide forward as you drop your rear end into the seat. This may be the only good way to get in from a dock in deeper water. (See Illustration # 5-1. Getting In.)

What do you do with your paddle while all this is going on? If you're leaving from a beach, just lean it across the boat in front of the cockpit and hope it doesn't float away. Or, find a nice paddle clip system and clip it in before you start. Talk to your dealer about paddle rests or clips. The most embarrassing moment for most novices (and some forgetful pros) is when you've stuck your paddle into the cockpit for carrying and forget to take it out before you enter. You'll find that taking out the paddle once you're halfway in is not a fun thing. This is where novices may take their first dunking (or mud bath in Florida) because you have to lean to one side, overbalancing the boat in a most unexpected way.

Many of the books written by experts tell you to place your paddle centered over the boat behind the cockpit while you grip the paddle with one hand on each side of the cockpit, including the sides of the cockpit. Use this grip as brace points for entry. It works particularly well with dock entries at about the same height as the boat. It's probably unnecessary and awkward in other situations.

A good exercise for first-timers, once you get into the boat and settled, is "rocking." Have someone hold the front of the boat loosely and rock the boat side to side to find the various turn-over points for that particular boat (don't go beyond them or that may be it for the day). One or two minutes of this does worlds of good for a new paddler's confidence because it shows you how much leeway you have before the boat will actually go over. Since this is usually a lot more than you think when you first sit in the tippy beast, it saves a lot of unnecessary overcompensation for lean and allows more concentration on paddling and direction. You can talk to people all day about primary and secondary stability, but it doesn't mean anything until they get in the boat and find out what that is. (Primary stability has been described as the amount you can lean to one side when you think the boat is going over but won't, secondary is the next level of lean where it will.)

2. Paddling

Moving the boat is what's important; the technique you use is less so. The more efficient you are, the more fun you'll have, and the easier it will be. There are a lot of paddling variations that may work for you. Paddling was taught to me by a whitewater instructor friend who was joining the ranks of sea kayaking in a whitewater boat. I unlearned some of what he taught, but the basics still hold true.

Initial placement. The center of the paddle should be kept over the centerline of the boat. The paddle centerline is the balance point between the two blades and is usually marked by the seam in the take-apart paddles. (The button that allows the paddle to come apart is never the middle).

Grip. Place your hands on each side of the center line, a little wider out than your shoulders (this allows you to push the paddle straight away from your shoulder rather than crossing over the boat each time). Grip comfortably with both hands, relaxed enough so that you can open one hand during the push part of your stroke as described below. Your thumbs should be under the paddle with the rest of your fingers curving around the top. For asymmetrical paddles, the longer part of the blade is usually uppermost. I'm not sure I know the reason for this, but that's the way the manu-facturers' names appear right side up. (See Illustration # 5-2. Paddle Handhold.)

Illustration # 5-2. Paddle Handhold

Motion. The basic motion was described to me as pedaling a bicycle with your hands, keeping the center line of the paddle over the center line of the boat at all times (except when you have to power stroke, correct stroke or brace, etc.). For long-distance stroking, avoid side-to-side shoulder movement as much as possible. Place one blade in the water a comfortable reach in front of you at as low an angle as you feel will fully cover the blade with water. White-water paddlers use a 45-degree paddle angle for speed. Sea kayakers should keep it much lower unless they need speed. Greenland Eskimo paddlers try to keep the pad-dle center as low to the boat as possible and take short strokes to minimize effort over long distances. It really doesn't matter as long as you have the energy to go where you want to. Once the blade is covered with water, push the upper hand until the blade is almost even with your body, then pull the bottom hand, giving a slight shoulder rotation in the direction of pull. The bottom blade of the paddle (in water) is taken out after it passes your body. Repeat on the other side. Try to have an even amount of push and pull on each stroke.

The general motion comes naturally, but the specifics for your stroke will take time. It took me two weeks to be able to paddle and look at the scenery without swinging the front of the boat back and forth 5' at every stroke. When you paddle on one side, the front of the boat turns to the other side. That's why you rush to paddle on the other side so you can counteract the motion and bring the boat in line. Most of your early paddling efforts will be just to go straight (or the direction you want to go) and you'll do it by quickly changing sides (as in a canoe) except the paddle is double-bladed and you won't have to shift hands. As you get more proficient, you'll make minor adjustments in the strength and length of each stroke, or blade orientation, to allow continuous even paddling. When you can keep the bow from moving more than 18" to 2' with each stroke, you're well on you way to a reasonable paddle stroke. Good paddling is much like a mantra that soothes your mind and body as you gracefully glide across water (see Illustration # 5-3. Paddling Technique).

3. Carrying

Carrying a kayak with two people is easy. One at each end and lift by the grab handles or ends of the boat. Carrying by yourself is a little harder. You can drag "Tupperware" boats over most types of ground and not worry about them. When you have to lift it by yourself, there are two good ways. One is to find the balance point around the cockpit and jerk the boat over your head with both hands and lower the boat with your head inside. Watch your feet and walk. The other way is to lift the kayak with your arm and shoulder inside the cockpit. The outside arm steadies and the inside shoulder becomes the balance point with the boat draped over your side. Wearing a good PFD with foam over the shoulder area helps cushion the weight. If there's a lot of wind, drag it or find a friend.

4. Safety

Rolling. Rolling is turning your boat 360 degrees with you in it. You use paddle pressure pushing on the water and hip movement to bring you back up. I've never learned how to roll. I tried once, and came close, but gave it up when I realized the type of water I was going into and the fact that you have to practice to maintain the skill. Rolling is a good safety skill. If you can learn it, do it. If you can't, don't worry much about it in Florida.

Illustration # 5-3. Paddling Technique

My reasons for not learning to roll are as follows. I'm too lazy. Most of the water I paddle is so shallow that if I tried to roll I would spend much of my time picking mud out of my teeth. The only rough water I paddle is surf and then only when it's warm and I have full shore support on a day trip just to try the surf. The water's rarely cold enough to make it important.

In eight years, the only time my boat went over outside of surf was when the boat was empty of camping gear and I paddled under a foot bridge. The top of the paddle got caught by a cross tie and I went over, into 10″ of water. I pushed up with my hand and continued on.

On the numerous group camping trips I've been on in Florida, there's been only one turnover. A hungry boater tried to pick up a scallop in a dip net in water that was too deep. As he reached down the current pulled the boat out from under him. He quickly recovered, pumped out his boat and we were on our way.

In order to practice rolling under real-life situations, you would have to expedition-pack your boat with internal and deck gear stowed. Since I can't trust the stuff to stay dry for the number of rolls I would have to try, I didn't even contemplate it. No one I know has ever rolled a fully loaded boat in Florida. These are my excuses. Read about rolling, find a good instructor and learn rolling and other safety techniques like bracing whenever you get the chance. It isn't necessary but it sure can make you more comfortable.

Bracing. Bracing is a way to keep your boat from turning over after it passes the point of no return but before your head hits the water. When you feel yourself falling over, you reach out with your paddle and slap the water, pushing yourself back up. It doesn't quite work that way but that's enough for this book. Read one of the technical kayaking books for a more complete explanation of high and low braces and practice, practice, practice. They are easy to learn and might come in useful some day.

Self Rescue. If you can't roll your kayak, there are a number of other rescue techniques you can use once the boat goes over. The easiest is to drag the boat to shore and dump out the water. If you can't do that, but are in shallow water, stand on the sea bottom and empty out your boat and get back in. If you have good bulkheads or flotation bags, you can empty the boat by getting to one side of the boat, turning the cockpit partially out of water, putting your shoulder under the boat behind or in front of the cockpit, and lifting slowly a few times. If it's really shallow, just pick up one end to drain. Much of the water will drain out. Get in the boat and sponge or pump out the rest. If you're in deep water, turn the boat over, get in and pump or sponge (and sponge and sponge) the water out. If you have a paddle float, put this on your paddle, secure it to the boat and use it for stability until you're ready to go on your way. Read about these in your technical kayak book. Practice them in warm water.

You should also practice "wet exits" (that's what paddlers do who go over and can't roll back up). Most people who have seen whitewater kayaking on TV are afraid they won't be able to get out of their kayak if it goes over. Unless you do something stupid like tie yourself in or get tangled with gear you shouldn't have stowed in the cockpit in the first place, this won't be a problem in a sea kayak. However, don't take my word for it. Do it and find out for yourself. Then you can practice all those neat self-rescue techniques you've read about. If you're smart, you'll always paddle with a buddy and you won't have to worry much about self rescue.

Group Rescue. If you paddle with a friend, group rescue techniques are the most effective. The more people you have, the more confusing and fun it can be. With two boats, it's simple. With three boats, it's embarrassingly easy. With four boats, it's a disaster. Here are two ways to do it with just you and another boat. For clarity, I'll call the boat that went over the "down" boat and the boat with the competent paddler the "up" boat.

When the boat goes over, the up boat paddles over while the brave kayaker hangs upside down under the down boat (sound like fun?). In other words, you hang upside down with your skirt still firmly attached and hold your breath. The up boat steers the bow of her boat into the down boat about midship near where the hands of the down boatman extend up out of the water by the cockpit (gently). When contact is made, the down boatman reaches up, grabs the bow of the up boat with one or both hands and pulls himself (and the boat) upright. This may sound a little complicated, but it is very easy if you keep your head and conditions are right. I have no idea how it will work under real conditions since it requires close paddling and an observant partner, but it's a breeze to practice.

The second technique requires a wet exit and will probably be used more often because when a boat goes over, the paddler usually gets out as fast as he can and then looks around for help. When the boat goes over and the down paddler wet exits, the up paddler (after she stops laughing) positions her boat so that the front of the down boat (upside down) is touching the up boat just in front of the cockpit at a 90-degree angle. The down paddler swims to the back of the down boat and starts climbing over the rudder (carefully!) and onto the stern bottom while the boat is still upside down. The up paddler grabs the front of the down boat and lifts it on top of her boat, pulling it across in front of her cockpit. As water leaves the down boat, it will be easier to pull. The purpose of the down paddler on the back of the down boat is to give it enough lift to allow the up paddler to pull it across. After a relatively short while, the down boat will be balanced over the up boat, upside down with most of the water out. The up paddler then turns it over and pushes it back into the water, grabbing the cockpit of the down boat (now up) and pulling it parallel to the up boat, cockpits matching. The up paddler grasps the two cockpits together for stability while the down paddler climbs in.

With three boats, the down paddler positions the down boat between the two up boats, making an "H" with the down boat acting as the cross piece. He can then help get one end up on one of the up boats or get out of the way. The up paddlers lift the down boat in front of both cockpits, emptying out the water. They then turn it over and return it to the water next to one of the boats. Finish like the single boat rescue above. (And don't put the down boat between the two when the water's emptied out. There is no way for the paddler to enter unless he crawls over a boat to get to his or slithers up from one end, banging his dangling legs as he moves. If both boats have to get into the finale, put the down boat on the outside and have the two up boats hand-lock cockpits with the down boat.) It's never quite this easy, but it's not that hard unless the waves and winds are bad.

There are all kinds of other rescue techniques and variations on the ones I've described, so be aware when you read other books. You will rarely, if ever, have to do this in Florida, but it's nice to know how ahead of time. Practice a few times with friends and remember.

Summary

Paddling and rescue techniques are important if you truly want to be safe and enjoy this sport. Fortunately, the boat and gear designs will keep you out of most trouble in Florida waters. Read up on these in a book written to inform you of the techniques, and practice or take lessons. None of these take much time and can add a lot to your understanding and enjoyment.

Chapter 6

CAMPING

Camping in Florida can be a wonderful experience, if you do it the right way, at the right time of the year and with the right equipment. Here are some general and specific hints for happy camping.

Probably the most important aspect of camping in Florida for your personal comfort is the time of the year. Bugs! Don't expect to enjoy camping after the middle of April and before the middle of October. I do my very best to avoid it during that time. December, January, and February are my favorites. I've included a bug section in this book, so refer to that if you want to know the details. Even during the preferred months, the bugs (especially no-see-ums and mosquitoes) can show up when the temperature warms into the 70s. The difference is that they disappear as the temperature drops in the evenings, and you can wear long clothing for protection. Bug repellent will work, but it will dissolve some of your favorite polypro and can become very old, very fast when you can't shower.

The correct way to camp on Florida's beaches is simple. Take everything you bring with you back with you. Don't disturb the shore vegetation and put your tent and cooking areas on sand, if possible.

No one has written a definitive work on body waste disposal in the Florida beach environment, so I'll make a few guesses. Carry out whatever you can. The camping spots on most coasts are few

Illustration # 6-1. Camping on the Big Bend Gulf Coast

and will be heavily used in the future. If you can't or won't carry out the solid human waste, bury it as far from the water as you can, at least 6″ deep. I presume it will decompose in time. See the Toilet Kits section in this chapter for some hints.

In Glacier Bay National Park in Alaska, we were told by the rangers to deposit all excrement in the intertidal zone where the water critters would see to its disposal. They probably did, over a long period of time, but it wasn't a nice sight at the few private locations near the water. The reason for using the intertidal was the inability of soil bacteria to do the decomposition necessary in the cold climes. That shouldn't be a problem in Florida, but I've seen no research in this area that answers the question. Use good judgment and respect for the next person using that site.

The same problem exists for disposal of kitchen wastes. I scatter mine over the water (salt water only). It's always gone by the next day. I don't want to use land disposal because it attracts too many animals who will become habituated to the site and a nuisance for campers in the future. I'll probably start carrying it out in baggies when my conscience catches up. Some of the established campsites in parks in north Florida have marvelous herds of skunks and raccoons that come out every night to feast on people's kitchen droppings.

The more remote sites on the coast have not been used often enough to support large populations of beach marauders. However, with more use, they will become a problem as well. Rock

Island, a remote island in the Big Bend area used by fisherman for many years, is a camping site we used in 1985. One member of our crew stored a loaf of bread inside his tent. The next morning, a few slices of bread were gone and a long rip was evident next to the bread's former location. Raccoon tracks were everywhere. Everyone else stored their food in their boats behind bulkheads to avoid this eventuality. Some learn harder than others. Remember, raccoons swim. Keep your campsites clean and your food protected.

Just a word about our predecessors on this land. Practically every area of higher coast land on the west coast and inland waterways were used by Native Americans for various purposes. They usually left behind remains that are easy to spot with a little looking (they weren't as clean as we intend to be). Don't pick them up. Leave them for the professionals.

Camping from a kayak is a little different from most other camping. It fits somewhere between backpacking and car camping. You need to put your gear into a limited space that's larger than a backpack but smaller than a car. Weight is a consideration but not all that high on the priority list. You almost always have to carry at least a two days' supply of water and that will ruin your weight controls. If you're comfortable with backpacking, you'll have no trouble with kayak camping. It's a wonderful transition. Get your gear ready for a backpacking trip and add 50 percent more luxuries. If you're a car camper or novice, read a good book on backpacking. The major difference for both is that you have to think about packing into cones of different shapes (front and back of boat) and through openings that may not match your folding.

1. Equipment

Camping with the right equipment can make the difference between fun and misery. In Florida, the weather is usually benign enough, and help close enough, that your mistakes won't kill you, but they can make for some rotten discomfort. There is equipment available in stores all the way from Kmart to the fancy outdoor specialty shop in the mall to outfit you appropriately. I like to mail-order it from the various catalogs. I like getting packages in the mail. I use the local stores to browse and touch, buying the newest thingy I just couldn't do without, right now.

My advice on camping equipment depends on how often you intend to camp and whether you want to use the equipment in other locations as well. I consider camping equipment like an investment in stocks and bonds. I buy the best I can afford and keep trading up. I camp a reasonable amount (ten days or more a year) from the mountains of the Northwest to the Florida coast. If you only intend to go once for an overnight, buy at Kmart. The stuff will do well enough. If camping is to become part of your life, buy the best you can afford.

Tents/tarps. A good high-quality tent is a pleasure indeed. It's easy to set up and will stay up even in a strong wind. It keeps the rain and bugs out and has enough room for you to store your night-time necessities. Because there are no bears to eat up your boat (as in Alaska), you can use the boat for storage of many items that you would otherwise bring into your tent or hang in trees. This will allow you to consider a smaller tent, or at least, a change in your food-control attitude. The best Florida tent is one that gives both good rain protection and ventilation so that it can be used during the day to get out of the sun and bugs. I own three tents, all of which are poor to horrible for Florida in the afternoon sun. I've never tried one of the tents with netting for top and sides, but it should work, as long as the fly covering doesn't inhibit the flow of air too much. Next time I might try putting my space blanket between the tent and fly if I have to use the tent in the sun. Maybe that will control some of the radiant heating that burns your brains out.

Don't worry about whether the tent is self-standing or not unless you expect to camp on chickees in the Everglades. You can always put stakes into a Florida beach. In fact, it might be worth your while to invest in some of the big sand stakes, because sand on some of the beaches is so unconsolidated in the upper layers that short stakes don't hold very well. Maybe that's a reason to buy a self-standing tent. I carry longer stakes for beaches so I've never had a problem.

The best shape for a tent is whatever suits you. We have one old pup tent that's no longer usable because the coating is peeling off the rainfly ($60), one tunnel tent that weights under 5 pounds that we use for backpacking ($450) and one dome tent that weighs in around 7 pounds that we use for kayaking and car camping (and let the kids carry backpacking) ($200). I like the dome best but appreciate the tunnel in heavy winds. When you get serious about buying a tent, read more about them and browse the catalogs.

The one piece of gear I consider a luxury, but worth taking along, is a kitchen tarp. It can make the difference between an experience and a nightmare. Its purpose is to keep off the rain while you cook, eat, and "transish." That last word means it will allow you to load and unload boats under shelter so you won't get water into the dry compartments of the boat or a dry tent. If it's raining when you come in to camp, you wait until it lets up and rush to put up your tarp. You then pull your boats under the tarp and wait for another dry (or drier) period and put up your tent. When you get ready to leave, reverse the procedure.

We spent four days and three nights on a trip where it rained more than 12″. We were dry and comfortable and had a super time. If we had not had our tarp, it would have been awful. I did have one bad experience when I needed to use the tarp for sun protection on a beach and the winds were gusting over 20 knots. My system of poles didn't work. I wonder if one of those beautiful, but expensive, para-wing tarps would work.

Sleeping bags/mats. Sleeping bags come in different materials, sizes, shapes and weights. The variations are for different conditions and different comfort preferences. You need a sleeping bag that will fit in the boat (compressible to a relatively small size), be warm enough for the temperatures (rated between +20 and +30 degrees for north Florida in the winter), and be stuffed with material that will still keep you warm even if wet. A high-quality goose down mummy bag fills all the requirements except one. It won't keep you warm if it's wet. You need some type of synthetic fill to do that. Unfortunately, most synthetics aren't as light or compressible. Though I've seen one recently advertised that is supposed to be equal to down, I've not had a chance to try it. Quallofil is the closest proven synthetic (though Lite-Loft may prove better). It's about 20 to 30 percent heavier than down and 25 percent less compressible. It retains 85% of its heat-holding capacity when wet, however. If I felt certain I could keep the down bag dry, I would use it all the time. As it stands now, I almost always use Quallofil for sea kayaking trips. At $100, it's also cheaper than down ($220+). As the years roll by, new technology will probably change all of these recommendations one way or the other. New materials are invented and names are changed. Get the camping catalogues and use common sense. Hey, if it suits you, use your old Sears pajama party bag with the bunnies on it. Whatever works.

Sleeping mats are just as important as bags as far as I'm concerned. A full-sized Therm-a-Rest pad is just like a hotel room (you wish). Actually, it's the finest invention since microchips.

A nylon-coated cover over open-celled foam that is self-inflating by leaving the valve open for a while. When you pack up, it compresses and rolls into a cylinder 3' or 4' in diameter and 24' long that fits right up into those pointy spaces in bow and stern. There are other types around, but this one has done it for me. I've slept on mine in hotel rooms and enjoyed the night's sleep. I wouldn't leave home without it.

There are acceptable lower-cost alternatives that work okay on Florida beaches: closed-cell foam pads and even no pad if the sand is warm and soft. I went on a six-day trip with a friend who brought along a full-sized blow-up mattress and a pump. He liked it even though he looked ridiculous pumping up his bed every night with an oversized high-volume raft pump.

Stoves/dishes/utensils. Always bring a camp stove with you. Though many places have available wood washed up on the shore, it wouldn't last long if everyone made fires to cook on. Besides, the remains are often messy and ugly if not cleaned up properly. If you do have a fire (nice to burn up trash), douse it when done and scatter the ashes out into the water unless there's a built-in fire ring. Keep the beach clean for the next person. Because there are no problems with cold weather and altitude, quick-light stoves like butane or propane are the easiest. I use a small backpacking stove if only two of us camp and a two-burner Coleman if more go. Whatever fits your packing scheme.

I was going to give you words of wisdom about dishes and utensils, but there isn't much here different than any other camping. I use Lexan spoons, plastic cups and stainless steel nesting pots. Use anything you have.

A wonderful thing to have with you on a kayak camping trip is a roll of paper towels. This may sound overly civilized, but they really make a difference. I usually take a roll and cut it in half so it fits in a Ziploc bag. It's amazing what uses you can find for them around the kitchen. And they burn easily.

Lights. In the winter it gets dark between 5:30 and 6:30 p.m., depending on the date. When it does, it's nice to have a little light. Flashlights are good, but a Coleman Peak 1 lantern with hard carrying case is the best, unless you like to carry those propane cylinders for the new propane lanterns. Someone brought a Coleman along on my first trip in 1985 and I haven't been without one since. The new propane lanterns may be as good, but I've never tried one so I don't know. I always take along a Mini-Mag flashlight with extra batteries as well. It's handy to buy one of the headbands or mouth holders for these if you read at night or wander around a lot.

Water bags/filters. There are some great water filters on the market. None of the ones within a reasonable price are worth much for coastal paddling in Florida because there is very little fresh, drinkable water near the coast. Though there are a lot of rivers, fresh water usually lies 4 to 6 miles inland, requiring an 8-to12-mile round trip to get questionable drinkable water. None of the water pumps that filter water work on salt water except for small amounts, and it usually destroys the filter. It's a lot easier to carry enough water for a few days and replenish at the towns and communities along the way. Even in the Big Bend area there are small stores where you can get water every 20 miles or so. The only place where you can't get water is Everglades National Park back country. You'll need enough for the whole trip.

I use the water bags sold at most camping supply stores. They're plastic bags inside a nylon cover and hanging strap with a rubber stopper that allows for water release and can be removed for filling. Buy new plastic bags after each camping season. Since there's no way to dry them out without reversing them, a tedious process that will usually cause a leak in any case, just buy a new one ($4.50). They're good because they hold 2 to 3 gallons and can be hung up on a tree for use as a water spigot. When they're empty, they fold up into a small handful and can be put away. They're also good for setting on the bottom of the boat for ballast. The only problem is that the rubber stoppers can be knocked off if you're not careful packing and handling. They also leak if you've used them too long. The leaks can be repaired with vinyl glue in an emergency. Always test them at home before you go.

If you don't want to invest in a water bag, use plastic jugs, plastic bottles of various sizes or anything that won't break easily and is small enough to fit in the boat. I went on an Everglades trip where one of the paddlers packed 30 plastic quart soda bottles with water. They were everywhere in the boat, but they worked.

Always carry a personal water bottle in the cockpit with you. I use a Nolgene plastic bottle in the quart or quart and a half size. Bicycle bottles work fine. Expect them to take some abuse, so recycled soda bottles probably won't last long. We did get a good deal on some 1.5-liter Evian and picked up ten as a treat. They worked well as cockpit bottles. Remember to leave an air bubble at the top. This will allow the bottle to float if it falls in the water.

Knives. I love knives. I must have ten or fifteen. There is no perfect kayak knife. If you expect to cut a lot of rope, get a serrated one. If you want something to do everything, get a big Swiss Army knife. Don't buy one of those neat steel-handled knives that look like a dagger and fit on your PFD. Whitewater folks may like these to cut lines when they get tangled up with trees and boulders, but I've owned one for nine years and never took it out of its case while kayaking.

When I camp out of my kayak I usually bring two knives: my Swiss Army knife for whittling and fixing things and my Gerber folding, lock back, fillet knife for cleaning fish and cutting food. If you want to carry only one knife, get the best you can for food preparation. Cutting onions, cheese, and bagels will be its primary occupation. I recently bought a Gerber pocket tool that's like a Swiss Army knife but has a pair of pliers built in. I left my Swiss Army knife at home and didn't miss it. I also left pliers and screw drivers at home as well. The Gerber worked fine and the pliers did come in handy. Use whatever works for you.

Netting/hats. Mosquito netting on your tent is important. Netted hats have their uses, but I'm always torn between various discomforts. I used a net hat once in Florida when the no-see-ums started biting and crawling into every orifice that was uncovered. It's very tough to eat that way. I usually remembered to lift the net the first few bites and then I drank cocoa right through the net. What a mess! I prefer to camp when there are no bugs, but since I can't always guarantee that, I usually bring one along even though I rarely wear it.

They also make net shelters that fit over you like a small tent. I used one to nap in one afternoon when I was stranded on an island by low tide. It worked. Since I have no intention of being that stupid again, I doubt if one will be high on my buy list. Unless it's really hot, you could climb into your tent just as easily.

Toilet kits. This section is included in anticipation of the future of coastal camping in Florida. As the recreation community finds out how terrific camping in Florida can be in the winter, there will be more and more problems with disposing of human waste. It's easy to overuse a fragile beach environment. The rafting trips using some of our major scenic rivers through national parks are required to pack out all human waste (of the solid variety, including used toilet paper). Their technique is simple and can be converted to kayak use on a small scale.

Use a small bucket and line it with a plastic bag. Pour in a small amount of Clorox from your handy small bottle and deposit your deposit, including used toilet paper. Remove the bag and secure it with a twist tie and place it in a secure holder such as an ammo box or airtight plastic Tupperware container. A small ammo box should hold eight to ten offerings safely. Dispose of the bags when you get home in an appropriate location. Most sea kayaks can hold these pieces of equipment without problems.

If you haven't reached this level of sophistication, just carry along a small plastic shovel and a roll of toilet paper in a large Ziploc bag.

2. Packing

Packing my boat for the first two or three times was very traumatic. There was just no way all that stuff was going to fit in. With careful planning (and an occasional discard), it did—and usually

with some room left over. The rule of thumb, if you're a back-
packer, is add 20 to 50 percent and you'll be okay. Another useful
rule is pack in small containers. Remember, you have those little
pointy ends that need to be filled up as well as places alongside
your feet and seat.

For most touring purposes, the weight in the boat (including
you) should generally be in balance. The boat is designed to paddle best that way. Conventional wisdom is that if you know you're
going to have a head wind, pack lighter in the front so the bow will
rise easily and the boat will go up and over the waves better. If you
expect a following wind, pack heavier in the front so the waves
coming over the back will more easily lift the stern. Unfortunately,
the shape of the front and back of your boat may have as much to
do with safe paddling under these conditions as how you distribute
the weight. One of my boats is great against a head wind and terrible with following seas. The way it's packed will make a difference, but not that much. Learn your boat before you worry too
much about shifting weight.

Packing containers. The brown plastic bag is the stock and
trade of all modern water travelers. It's cheap, easy to find, small
to pack and waterproof if cared for very gently. I use these when I
forget my high-tech bags or the high-tech bags leak. I also use
them for redundancy backups inside the waterproof bulkheads that
leak a little (or someone drips into them). They may not work for
long trips unless you use a technique shown to me by a paddling
partner. Buy uncoated nylon stuff sacks of various sizes (look for
any reasonable quality). Put the plastic bags inside the nylon bags.
Seal the necks and close the nylon bag with the drawstring. Unless
you tear the plastic bags somewhere or water gets in the neck of
the bag, this works relatively well. It also makes packing easier
because these bags can be so much more stuffable in those strange
spaces. Even multiple plastic bags without the nylon sack covers
have been known to leak. I have been on trips where the sleeping
bags were covered with three or four bags and still got a little wet.

One of the finest inventions for kayak camping is the flotation storage bag for boats without bulkheads. These cone shaped
bags fit in the front and back of the boat, open at the big end to
allow gear storage, and seal water tight. Once sealed, they can be

blown up through the long tubes with valved ends that come attached to each. (See Illustration # 6-2. Flotation Storage.) When you camp, you pull out the storage bag and drag it up onto the beach. Because it's waterproof, you can leave it out of the tent until the next morning. Flotation storage bags act like little one-drawer dressers. A note of caution about packing them into the boat: Make certain that the valves are open so the compressed air can be released. If you don't do this, you may pop the bags along a seam. Once the bag is in place you can blow it up to fill the spaces and then close the valves.

Flotation storage comes in vinyl or coated nylon material. Vinyl is the cheapest ($50 for two) while the heavier grade of coated nylon is by far the best ($90 for two). I've owned six pairs of vinyl bags and all have come apart. I stopped using them. I repaired each a few times before giving up. They won't take the compression necessary to squeeze them into the boats. The coated nylon ones may also develop holes, but they are easier to patch. I've had one minor leak in five or six trips with the good bags.

There are also a number of wonderful waterproof storage bags of all sizes, shapes, and materials. The newest have waterproof zippers. I don't own one of these but I do have one or two of every other kind (we have a friend who's a manufacturer's representative). Most of mine have the roll-down-and-snap-buckle closures though a few have the chamber-of-horror slide tubes. They all work well unless you don't use them properly. They will leak a little if totally submerged for any length of time but do fine for the normal splashes and boat water. Buy at least one so you look like a kayaker. Besides, you need something to keep your spare jacket and lunch dry.

I also own a couple of those big canoe bags that have carrying straps for portaging (I got such a deal!). Anyway, I really do use them on my kayak camping trips. They've turned out to be perfect for on-deck storage of those items I don't want to put inside, or can't fit. They become the depository of the wet and dirty as the trip progresses. The tent, tarp, stove, fuel bottles, and lantern go in there, along with any chairs that aren't being used in the cockpit. They can be strapped on with bungee cords at an appropriate location (usually behind the cockpit), depending on weight needs and attachment points. This may cause some problems with crosswinds but you are shielded by your body from head winds. I've never had a problem with them secured on deck.

Map cases come in a number of sizes and shapes that are pretty handy. I used to use a sturdy vinyl Ziploc case that's notebook paper size and large enough for my small compass. It lasted five or six years. The edge under the closure tore and allowed water to leak in. I also found the closures a bit balky. Some of the more expensive skirts have clear map pockets built in that look interesting if you intend to wear a skirt all the time. A good gallon freezer Ziploc is probably good enough, particularly if you have those expensive, waterproof charts.

Camera containers are also important if you intend to bring anything but a waterproof camera. They come in blow-up, soft, waterproof bags, waterproof pouches and hard cases of all sizes and shapes. I carry my old Nikon and lenses in a soft waterproof bag with a little padding inside. I usually store it between my legs in the boat where I can get to it in a reasonable period of time. The area is always wet, so good bag construction is a must. I once owned a blow-up pouch but never felt comfortable with it. It always seemed too bulky and hard to get into when I needed the camera fast. I've also used a hard box that had to be stored on deck but discovered everything got too hot there during the day and the box was too big to fit inside. If you have a good camera, it's worth buying a good waterproof container that fits your needs.

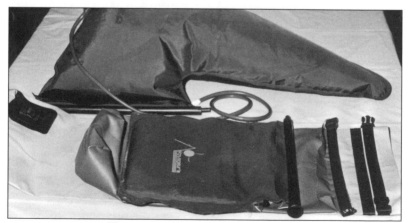

Illustration # 6-2. Flotation Storage

3. Miscellaneous Camping Hints

• Rolled up Therm-a-Rest mattresses fit well in the pointy ends, as do fuel and water bottles.

• Stuff your sleeping bag in its stuff sack and then into a plastic bag, or put the plastic bag in the stuff sack first and then stuff the bags. Try compression stuff sacks if you can afford them.

• If you have to shove your bags way up into the point of the boat and you have no hatches to make access easier, attach different colored ropes to them so you can retrieve them easily.

• Pack your dry shore shoes last, on top of the inside load facing up. This way you can wear your dry shoes as long as possible and get them out as soon as you need them at night. By facing them up, you get the boat, not the gear, dirty.

• Plan to carry a small waterproof storage bag or box on deck or in the cockpit with you for Band-Aids, flares, matches, sun blocker, lip ice, bug stuff, whistle, knife, spare toilet paper, short length of rope and flashlight. These are things you may need while paddling or immediately upon hitting shore.

• Pack your new boat once the night before you go, if possible. I did this on my first trip. It helped a lot. It didn't make me totally comfortable since I added forgotten items at the last minute, but it reduced my pre-trip terror to mild trauma. Once you know it all fits, then think about the most efficient packing.

• Use a camping list that you modify after each trip. (See Appendix 4.) I've used the same one each time with modifications that fit the upcoming circumstances. Since it's on my computer, I just print the changed version. I check the list at least twice. Once to make sure I've got everything I need and the second time to make sure the items are in the "to stow" pile. I also prepare a food list based on the number and types of meals I expect.

• When you get to shore for the night, set up your tent and prepare your bedding and clothes before dark. Put the stove, pots, and utensils near the food. Then go play. I hate to set up camp in the dark when I'm tired and cranky.

Summary

This whole chapter is a summary. Reread it if you can't remember what it says.

Chapter 7

FISHING

For those of you interested in obtaining your own food from the wild while kayaking, I am including this chapter as a brief guide. It's not intended to be definitive, or even good, but just a few words to help you make the transition from other places to Florida and sea kayaks. There are more books on fishing in Florida than on how to cook pasta. Go buy one or a recent fishing magazine. A note of caution: Unless you're willing to eat some very weird stuff, don't depend on what you can catch for your primary food supply. An overactive commercial fishing industry, loss of habitat and too much pollution has made Florida waters uncertain, at best, for dependable food gathering. This is particularly true during the winter months in the central and northern part of the state.

Florida requires a saltwater fishing license for fishing from a boat in salt water. This applies to people carrying fish in a boat even though they've actually done their fishing from land (unless they're very convincing). I don't take chances because even if I can beat the rap, the time involved makes the license worthwhile. Resident licenses are cheap ($12) and short-term out-of-state licenses ($5 three-day, $10 week, and $30 annual) are also. When you get the license, find the newest list of regulations. There are seasons and bag limits for most species.

Fishing from a kayak should be a new experience for most of you. Like other new experiences, it has its good and bad points. The good points are accessibility to coastal waters unreachable by most other craft, quiet, non-polluting transportation, low cost, and a sense of freedom hard to find any other way. The bad points are a small range to fish, cramped storage space, a fair amount of physical effort to get where you're going and a limitation on the size of fish you can safely land (rarely a problem).

You also have to learn a few new techniques. First, you have to figure out what you need to bring along and where you can put it so it's all available to you when you need it. Second, you need to remember how to paddle with all that stuff all over your boat. Third, you need to think about what's going to happen if you really do catch something. How do you land the fish and not turn over? I'm not sure I have the answers to these questions, since every boat is a little different, but I'll try with a few.

Once you read the local paper, fishing guide or magazine that tells you what's available and where to get it, that should help you with the gear problem. Fishing in each area of the state is very different. Winter fishing is okay in the south but very poor inshore in most of the north. Summer fishing can be relatively good all over. Certain species will stay around the waters you can reach, others just move through. Wandering around the coastal fishing spots and talking to people, as well as checking with local bait shops and marinas, can help a lot. Just remember, a motorboater's description of mileage is in no way related to kayaker's reality. Don't ever believe "it's just a mile or so up the way." If they can't point it out on a map or chart, expect that mile to be anywhere from 1 to 10 miles.

1. Gear

Here's my usual fishing gear list for day trip fishing.
- One short rod with reel (I prefer open spinning).
- A tackle box with appropriate gear, either the standard 14" x 8" x 8" or a flat 6" x 4"x 2."
- One crab net.
- One or two cast nets (one for bait).

- One knife and a pair of needlenose pliers in cases on a belt around my waist.
- One bait bucket.
- One diver's net bag for live fish storage.
- One cooler as large as the boat will safely handle (with ice, drinks and lunch), strapped on the deck.
- Fishing license.
- My normal kayaking safety gear.

2. Critters to Catch

Florida waters contain a lot of sea life that's good to eat. Fish are the usual but other goodies abound as well. Since most of your paddling will be inshore, that's what I'll stick to. Common fish species you should think about catching include: redfish (red drum), spotted sea trout, flounder, snook (special tag), sheepshead, Spanish mackerel, rock bass, mangrove snapper (and other snappers), bluefish, and mullet.

Blue crabs are abundant in most areas if you know how to catch them and you're willing to work a little. There are two usual ways to catch these crabs without a trap. The first is to actively fish them with a chicken neck or fish head tied to a string tossed into a deeper hole and gently pulled in once bites are felt until you can scoop them up in your crab net. The second, and the preferred method for active kayakers, is to walk the shallows with your bow line tied to your belt, scooping up whatever crabs appear. Once caught they are tossed into the cooler after removing or protecting your lunch. I do this on my way to my local fishing hole up the salt creek on the low-energy west coast. Mud conditions may make this difficult in some areas.

Bay scallops are the jewel of Florida's west coast. The season opens in July and closes in September, but you might stumble on a few through December (don't even think of picking up a few and putting them in your spaghetti sauce when they're out of season). Some years they're there, some years not. When they're in, they are really in. The best way to get them is to put on snorkeling gear and swim through the grass beds, looking for the shape or fluorescent blue eyes staring at you. Grab them and stick them in your diver's bag. There have been times when I reached my limit in an hour and shucked for the rest of the day. Check with the locals before you try to get scallops. Sometimes they're further off shore than you want to go, other times they're just not there. The most consistent runs seem to be in the southern Big Bend area and St. Joseph Sound in the Panhandle, though they can appear anywhere on the west coast. If you don't want to get out of your boat, you can retrieve scallops with dip nets or by just walking in shallow water when the tide is right. The scallop regulations are scheduled to change in 1994, so look at the regulations when you get your license.

Oysters are plentiful throughout Florida but few are safe to eat. Check with the Florida Department of Environmental Protection to find open areas. The Big Bend and Apalachicola Bay are the few places where there are locations that are open most of the time, but cold water months are safer. I stopped eating raw oysters because of the possible contaminants and bacteria. Suit yourself.

Clams can be found in a number of places around the state, some by shuffling your feet along the bottom and others by digging in the right mud banks. I've used the first method but was never successful with the second. Locals can give you the best information. Always check for local health warnings with appropriate officials. Do not trust the locals for this since some of the short-lived ones ignore the warnings.

Florida lobsters are even better than bay scallops, but their range is more restricted and they're harder to find unless you get to the right places early. Most of the shallow-water lobsters are in the southeast part of the state, mainly the Keys. Their season starts August 1 and they are usually taken by diving. A special $2 stamp is required. They're found mostly in cracks in the coral or rock canals, though sometimes you'll see them walking on the grass beds. Check local conditions if you get serious about lobsters.

Skates and rays are often caught while fishing for other species, particularly in the shallow bays. If someone tells you "they taste just like scallops" or "unconscionable restaurants plug the wings to cheat customers into thinking they're really scallops," don't believe them. Most rays are edible, but they can't be mistaken for scallops by a long shot. Rays have long strips of cartilage in their wings about every 1/4″ that run perpendicular to their bodies. Between these are nice, small strips of flesh that are about the same flavor as shark. Actually pretty tasty stuff, but scallops they ain't! Fishermen should leave sharks and rays alone. They're fairly common now but are being depleted rapidly by newly established commercial fisheries. They reproduce slowly and probably cannot support a sustained yield.

There are a lot of edible exotics in the southern part of the state, but I'm not very familiar with their abundance or safety. These include sea urchins, sea cucumbers and various sea weeds. I can give no advice here.

3. Fishing Rods

A short rod is very important. It's too hard to handle a long one from the boat. If you really like the longer poles, get one you can take apart in two or more pieces in order to carry it safely. If you intend to do more than day trips, pick one that won't rust if left unwashed around salt water for long periods. Since fresh water will be at a premium, don't expect to do much cleanup until you come back to port. I use a small spinning reel for the same reason. Over the last few years a number of outfitters have been offering rod holders that attach to the boat in various locations. These are very handy if you want to troll while paddling (or read a book while waiting for the fish to bite).

4. Nets

I always bring two and sometimes four nets. The crab net can also be used as a landing net under some circumstances, so my landing net is usually left home unless I intend to be in deeper water and don't expect to do any crabbing. Crab nets or landing nets can be used for scallops as well. They're usually cheap ($4 to $5) and don't last very long.

My most important net is my bait cast net. A lecturer at a recent sea kayaking symposium for the Southeast claims that as long as he has his 4'-radius cast net, he can always catch something for the pot. If you're willing to eat small fish, he's probably right. The main purpose of the smaller cast net is to catch minnows so you can catch bigger fish. I've always caught bait and was sometimes able to catch bigger fish with the bait. Using the net at low tide when the baitfish clump up is the smartest time. I also have an 8′ net that I use for bigger fish, such as mullet, which should be around all year. I don't use this much because I've never learned to throw it as well as I would like.

5. Traps

You can purchase shrimp and crab traps that can be tended from a kayak with a little ingenuity or placed up the sloughs where the bigger boats can't go. I've never used traps but know others who have. Don't expect to take them with you on any overnights.

6. Bait

You can use artificials, catch your own bait with a cast or dip net or buy it before you leave the dock. They all work if you're in the right place at the right time. Live shrimp is the best (and most expensive) and fingerling mullet and pinfish a close second. Most live minnows work but some don't stay on the line very long. Weedless spoons (and hooks) are important for kayak fishing because most of it will be near shore in grass beds or rocky artificial channels.

7. Information Resources

The public library, local newsstand, the Internet, and bait and tackle shops are your best information resources. After these, talk to people who are fishing on bridges and beaches and getting out of boats at marinas. Local newspaper reports are also helpful but usually a day or two late. Explore on your own and try a place that seems right. Since you can go places most others don't, you can never tell what you'll catch.

One last personal note. I found it very difficult to fish and camp during the same trip if I expected to pack up and move every night. There was just not enough energy or daylight hours to do both. It was also hard to clean off the blood and guts without fresh water. Since winter is not the best time to fish in North Florida, I usually don't bother any more. If I haven't tried to fish on a camping trip in a while I usually try it once and give it up. The exception was a trip to Glacier Bay in Alaska, where we hit a run of silver salmon by luck and had a great dinner with wild strawberries. Now, of course, that's a good enough run of luck to never give up the dream, but since I had mine, I don't need it any more.

Summary

The best fishing in most of Florida is in the summer and the best camping in the winter. Unless you have a lot of time, plan to day-trip for fishing and forget it when you take extended trips in the north and central areas unless you have no time constraints and can afford to do a lot of fish searching.

Chapter 8

FLORIDA GEOGRAPHY:
GENERAL SHAPE & COASTLINE

The reason Florida should be so exciting to sea kayakers is water. There's a lot of water out there. Depending on who you believe, there are over 8,000 miles of coastline to explore. Add the intercoastal systems and you have some real distances to test your mettle against or to amble along. This chapter will discuss the regional geographical differences and the types of paddling available in each area.

1. Regional Coastal Differences

If you're new to Florida, buy a *Florida Atlas and Gazetteer* at the local bookstore and use it for a general planning guide. It contains small-scale maps of the state in book form at 1:150,000. It's best for telling you how to get where you want to go rather than what to do when you get there. The U.S. Coast Guard nautical charts at 1:80,000 seem to be the most useful overall, though I've used larger-scale quad maps from time to time for more careful exploring. Because of changing conditions in the coastal areas, these large-scale maps can be misleading from the vantage point of a kayaker, so be careful if that's all you have. Local engineering supply houses have the most diverse map collections, but some bookstores and office supply stores also keep a few. Bait and tackle stores will probably have your nautical charts. (See Illustration # 8-1. Florida's Coastal Segments.)

Illustration # 8-1. Florida's Coastal Segments

St. Marys River to Cape Canaveral. The Atlantic shore from the state border at the St. Marys River to Cape Canaveral is typified by a continuous stretch of sandy beaches broken only by occasional inlets and river outflows, including Florida's largest, the St. Johns River. The Atlantic Intercoastal Waterway runs inland from the beaches a few miles.

The Atlantic is often rough and unpredictable with high surf at various times of the year. The winter months and periods with major off-shore storms are usually the worst. During the normal summer weather patterns the mornings can be almost calm with gentle swells. Unless you are an experienced paddler, I wouldn't consider this stretch of coast except for day paddles, with an alternative in mind if the weather doesn't work out. The beaches are sandy and wide but developed in most areas. All the beaches are public, but camping is usually prohibited by local ordinance. The best way to experience this shoreline is to pick out a nice park with beachside campsites or a motel and play in the surf. Multi-day trips are good only for the experienced paddler who is willing to risk the surf with a full boat and plan very carefully. There are many motel rooms along this stretch of coast if you can't find the right park or don't want to camp. Watch out for rocks and jetties along inlets and artificial sand traps fruitlessly trying to save eroding beaches from Mother Nature. Tides may expose a few rocks along the shore and cause unusual rips and rough waters at most inlets.

The safest overnight trips along this coast are in the Intercoastal Waterway. The waterway is fairly wide along most of its length, with numerous salt creeks coming in from both sides. Though there's a stretch south of St. Augustine that's man-made, the rest follows natural bodies of water behind the main coastal barrier islands. There are quite a few big boats using the Intercoastal but I haven't found them to be much trouble because of the width of the water systems. The Intercoastal on the east coast has much in common with the low-energy shore of the Big Bend area: lots of salt creeks and broad marshes, muddy shores, oysters, and sea life, dotted with occasional higher hammock areas. There are fewer, if any, natural sand beaches, however, and most of the land is not available for camping. Since it's not open to the ocean except at the inlets, there are fewer breezes and a lot more bugs. It's also more developed than the Big Bend.

The inlets and rivers north of the St. Johns may prove to be a very fertile kayaking area as soon as someone takes the time to inventory the camping resources and draw some good maps. If you include Cumberland Island National Seashore, this could become a very exciting winter destination. With two federally owned recreation sites, a number of new state land purchases and a county park, camping areas should increase and make extended overnights possible.

The upper part of the Intercoastal is mostly juncus and spartina marshes (tall grasses) and the southern part of this section begins to intersperse mangrove trees with the grasses. Each type of vegetation provides different challenges for the paddler. You could spend a lifetime along the Intercoastal and its tributaries and not see half of the places it could lead you. However, because of development and pollution, there are a lot of places you wouldn't want to go. The Trips section of this book gives a few hints but the Florida Atlas and Gazetteer can show you places to discover and explore.

Cape Canaveral to Ft. Lauderdale. This area of the state has similar water systems to the area to the north but with very different weather and water conditions. Until recent times this area was relatively unpopulated along the water. Unfortunately, Florida's big growth spurt of the last 30 years took care of that.

The Atlantic coast in this area has sandy beaches like the northern parts of the state but the energy levels are lower. This means that the beaches and waves are smaller. There are also a few more rocky areas along the beaches where the limestone layers have been exposed by beach erosion. Beach camping is prohibited in most areas, but beachside parks are relatively common. Though the surf is rarely as rough as the areas north, it can still be quite challenging.

The intercoastal vegetation changes to mostly mangrove trees with a few salt marsh areas. The development patterns have left some areas to explore but not anywhere near the amount to the north. Look for parks and wildlife refuges. The farther south you go the fewer natural areas are left.

Ft. Lauderdale to Miami. This area is good for urban paddling. The surf has gentled and the fast boats have increased substantially. You can always find a peaceful area to paddle but you have to look a little harder. If you're used to the Hudson River in New York, this will seem like a tropical paradise. If your home territory is the San Juan Islands or the offshore Maine islands, you probably won't stay around here long.

Biscayne Bay National Park and the Florida Keys. South from the Miami area is a whole new world. Biscayne National Park is relatively unspoiled with a lot of open water and a few islands that can be explored. Check with the park to find out what facilities are available. It's changing to meet existing needs. Concessionaires in the park may be willing to help with your transportation to outlying areas. The Florida Keys further south are a world unto themselves. The islands along the highway are highly developed except in a few locations. Commercial camping facilities and some park camping is available, though very crowded during the winter months. The unbridged islands are usually undeveloped and privately owned and there a lot of these. A few may be suitable for camping, but a lot of planning needs to be done before you expect to do extensive camping in the Keys.

The Atlantic coast can be a little rough from time to time but is rarely a problem for kayakers. That's where the tropical reefs are. Bring masks and snorkels for some breathtaking underwater views. The better reefs are a little too far out for the average paddle; however, there are small patch reefs next to shore that have some of the same critters in smaller quantities. The Florida Bay waters inland are also exciting to explore and safer to paddle in most instances. They are loaded with undeveloped little keys that are typified by mangroves with occasional small beaches. Many are underwater at high tide. Remember, except for a passing rainshower or a faucet, there is no available potable fresh water in the Keys.

Everglades National Park and Upper Florida Bay to Ft. Myers. This area has the best tropical saltwater paddling in Florida. The Everglades National Park has a long history of catering to paddlers. There are a number of great trips in the park if you want a tropical experience. See the Trip section of this book or write the park for more details.

The waters north of the park are very similar to the park without the park protection. The further north you get, the more the areas are developed and the rougher the surf on the Gulf side. However, the surf is almost never a problem during normal weather patterns. The beaches on this side of the state are usually narrow, more crushed shell than sand, have few high dunes, and are often surrounded by tall condominiums once you get to Marco Island and Naples. The shoreline away from the beaches is usually mangrove trees and muddy. There are a number of bays and estuaries that are very good paddling areas, particularly if you want to look at wildlife or fish. Rookery Bay National Estuarine Sanctuary is a good place to start once you leave the Everglades.

Ft. Myers to Sarasota. The Gulf surf in this area is not much different from the area to the south (or to the north) nor are the beaches. (Both surf and beaches are pretty much the same until you get north of Bayport). There are a number of internal and external paddle opportunities with some commercial and park camping. However, any extended trips would have to be well planned because of the coastal development.

Tampa Bay. I've listed Tampa Bay separately because it's a large body of water with some very interesting urban paddling and wilder areas in the southeast portion. If you intend to visit the area, you can always find somewhere pleasant to paddle. The shorelines are low energy in most places but the waves can build quickly along the causeways.

St. Petersburg to Bayport. This area is much like the area to the south. Highly developed on the coast with lots of inland paddling opportunities. There are also a few offshore islands and parks near land that are fun to visit. Check the outfitters in the area.

Bayport to the Suwannee River. This is the beginning of north Florida's wilderness camping. Once you pass Bayport, the Gulf beaches become spotty and the salt grass marshes begin to pre-dominate. This is the only area near the coast of Florida where you can get fresh water from springs and small streams. However, you still have to paddle up quite a ways and I would only use these in an emergency. This is the area that should be the beginning or ending of a long Big Bend paddling trip. There are lots of opportunities for day trips and overnights, but it's the easiest area in the state to find both wilderness and safe paddling. The beaches are low energy, and most of the shoreline is mangroves and marsh in the south to grassy marsh in the north. Large expanses of mud flats are exposed at low tides, and you can always escape from large waves by going closer to shore. There is very little surf to speak of along this part of the coast.

Suwannee River to the Ochlockonee River. This is my coast. It's the area I've paddled the most and is the least-developed area except for the Everglades. There are lots of places to camp outside of established parks or campgrounds. The development is usually weekend homes built behind the salt marshes except for the occasional fishing villages. Water sources and small groceries are usually around 20 miles apart with enough camp spots in between to make things fairly easy. This area is covered in detail in Chapter 15.

Ochlockonee River to St. Joseph Bay. From the mouth of the Ochlockonee River south and around the point, the coastal topography changes dramatically. The shoreline once more becomes high-energy with sandy beaches and sand dunes. The beaches themselves are a cross between the Atlantic and Gulf beaches further to the south. Less sand than the Atlantic and less shell than the Gulf. They're about as wide as the other Gulf beaches with slightly rougher wave action. These beaches are limited to the barrier islands and the outer points of the mainland, except for a few places like Turkey Point.

The water behind the barrier islands can be smooth or rough depending on weather conditions and size. There are beaches along the bay side of some of the islands, interspersed with a fair amount of marsh. The mainland part of this coast is mainly U.S. 98 and its accompanying development. There are some small motels, stores and restaurants that can be used by the paddler in planning long trips in this area. Pre-scouting is recommended because the lives of these enterprises seem to be short.

The vegetation changes dramatically along the northern coast. Pine plantations now reach the shore with only interspersed areas of marsh grasses along the stream and river entrances.

There are a number of camping opportunities along this coast, including state parks, commercial campgrounds, and a few private beaches. Dog Island is closed to camping unless you know a friendly landowner, and St. George Island is limited to designated areas within the park. St. Vincent's Island is a federal national wildlife refuge that allows camping only during certain times of the year with special permission. Check with the refuge office for information on this. St. Joseph Bay State Park allows camping at designated camp spots as well as some wilderness camping.

St. Joseph Bay State Park is probably the best area of the state for beach camping and exploring. Though portions of the barrier islands and barrier spits are developed, much are in parks or preserves. There are times of very rough water along the Gulf beaches so trips need to be planned carefully.

St. Joseph Bay to Perdido Bay. The remaining beaches in Florida offer a lot of good paddling within a more developed context. Though there are still some wonderful camping opportunities, they have to fit around the military bases and population centers. Panama City, Ft. Walton Beach, Pensacola, and all the smaller towns in between use up a lot of beach. There are, however, a number of parks and commercial camping facilities along the way and the beach systems are very similar to the beaches to the east. A few of these beaches have been rated among the world's best with deep blue waters and glaring white sands. They're always worth a try.

The inland water systems are also similar in vegetation and wave action to the areas further east. Exploring the nooks and crannies of the bays could keep you occupied all winter. Many parts of the bays and Intercoastal Waterway are still undeveloped. There are few directions in the literature about these areas, so I would suggest that you do a lot of map reading, road work and short paddles before you do extensive trips.

Summary

The Florida coastline is very diverse: high-energy and wide beaches in the northeast to flat water in the Everglades. Choose the area carefully and you can't miss a paddling experience to remember.

1. Spring Creek

2. St Marks Lighthouse (top)
3. 1985 Expedition Portrait (left)
4. Pinhook River (right)

5. **Bowlegs Point** (right)
6. **Dallus Creek Stopover** (bottom)

7. Camping, Apalachicola River

8. Pulling through mud at Jug Island. (top)
9. Suwannee River — Big Shoals (bottom)

10. Flamingo pre-packing (top left)
11. Camping on Lazy Island (top right)
12. Pepperfish Keys — typical marker (bottom left)
13. D. Gluckman in fishing regalia (bottom right)

4. Camping,
   Apalachicola
   River (top)
5. Keaton Beach
   (bottom)

16. **Steinhatchee** (top)
17. **St. Marks Lighthouse** (bottom)

Chapter 9

WEATHER PATTERNS AND TIDES

Weather Patterns. Florida has diverse weather patterns that change with location and time of year. They are influenced by winter frontal systems from the north, hurricanes from east, south and west, and summer storms from practically any direction. Since there are no mountains in the state (the highest point is under 400'), the major geological feature impacting the weather is the land-water interface along the coast. Once you understand a little about the weather in the area you intend to paddle, you can be fairly certain of the weather conditions within a reasonable range. The NOAA weather radios blanket the state with fairly accurate information that can be refined with the use of local television radar. You should have at least 12 hours' warning of any unusual weather except for specific thunderstorms. These you just have to look out for as you paddle and take shelter where you may.

Winds. Florida wind patterns are surprisingly constant during many parts of the year. In the summer, the winds are off the shore in the morning and on shore in the afternoon. They rarely get over 20 knots and are often calm to 5 knots. The normal wind is 8 to 12 knots. During thunderstorms the winds can blow 35 to 50 knots for short periods. If you have any indication there will be tornadoes or hurricanes, just stay away from the coast. The winds can be over 200 knots. They can kill you.

In the winter, the winds usually depend on the frontal systems coming from the northwest or northeast. They can be as high as 25 to 35 knots as the front passes. The winds move around the compass as the front approaches and goes through. The wind will blow from the east and southeast as temperatures begin to warm. As the front approaches, the wind shifts to the south with more warming. Just before the front comes through, the winds will pick up and shift to the southwest and west, along with rain. When the front passes, the wind continues to increase and shifts to the northwest and north while the temperature drops and the air clears. The long cold spells will have three or four days of northerly winds before they shift around to east again. Some fast-moving fronts only have a few hours of northerlies.

Winter winds in the south part of the state may be surprisingly constant for long periods of time. I paddled out of Flamingo in Everglades National Park one February when the winds were 18 to 25 knots from the east and southeast for five days straight. When I got back, the rangers told us the wind had been blowing like that for the last two weeks. We later learned that they continued for the next two weeks. Apparently, this was not unusual for that time of the year.

Spring and fall patterns are a combination of summer and winter patterns except that late summer and early fall have the most hurricanes. These will screw up any expected wind patterns.

If you have a good weather report, you can usually predict the wind direction and velocity for any day paddle. However, planning coastal trips by predominant wind direction (at your back all the time) just doesn't seem to work well. The wind is too subject to local conditions and the coastline, except along the east coast, has too many sinuosities. Even though you may generally be going north or south, you may spend almost as much time paddling east and west to get around coastal features. I try to have a general knowledge of wind conditions before I paddle and deal with what happens when I get there. I don't paddle if I know winds are going to be higher than I want to handle. Since that's rarely the case in most areas of Florida, wind usually doesn't determine my paddles.

Rain. Florida is not Alaska. It doesn't rain all the time. Some of you may not believe that, but it's true. The average rainfall is around 55 inches a year with almost half of that in big storms or fronts. The dry season is usually during the fall in the central and south and in the spring in the north. Winter rains are usually associated with frontal systems and summer rains are usually of the daily shower/thunderstorm pattern. There are some summer fronts and there are some winter thunderstorms. Local weather reports are usually fairly accurate in predicting rain in the short range. There are too many variables for much accuracy long range. It is very rare to have extended periods without sunshine in most of the state (one newspaper used to give free papers if the sun didn't shine within 24 hours). In the summer you may have 30 to 40 days where it rains every day, though mornings or afternoons will probably be sunny.

Rain can come down in gentle drizzles or like monsoons. Be prepared, bring rain gear and watch your local cable radar.

Heat/cold. Florida stays mostly tropical in the south and temperate in the north. In the summer, the temperatures along the coast are about the same statewide: low 70s in the mornings to upper 80s during the afternoon. Move these temperatures up about 5 to 8 degrees if you're in a developed area or inland. Water temperature is a major factor, ranging from the low 70s at the beginning of the summer to the mid 80s by September. Shallow creeks and inlets can be even hotter.

In the fall, the first frost shows up in late October in the north and some years not at all in the south. If frost does make it south, it's usually from mid-December through February. Florida winter temperatures are more stable in the south than in the north. In the Miami area, expect winter high temperatures in the 60s and 70s, while in the north drop that ten degrees. Lows in the south rarely reach the 40s while the mid-20s is not uncommon for the north.

The best way to describe Florida weather in the winter for campers is to consider north Florida like summer in the Rockies and south Florida like summer in upstate New York. You can get some cold weather but mostly it's fairly comfortable. In Florida in the summer, figure you're in the tropics. Dress cool and protect yourself from the sun.

There are exceptions to these generalities. It has been below zero in north Florida and in the 20s in Miami. It has also been in the 90s in Tallahassee in December. It doesn't happen often, but it does happen. Your local weather station will help you know when to expect these unusual conditions.

Waves. The description of regional geography in Chapter 8 gives some general wave conditions in various areas around the state. The Big Bend and the Everglades have the smallest, the upper east coast the largest and the rest are in between. All are negotiable by experienced kayakers except during storms or northeasters. I saw 15-footers breaking a quarter of a mile from the beach with crazy cross-breaks and backups during one storm. Usually the bigger surf is under 5 feet and the smaller surf on the west coast isn't. If you intend to paddle the surf, learn its secrets. Know the different types of waves and other sea features like runouts, underwater sandbars and undertows so that you can handle them appropriately.

Because there are few rocks on the beaches, the payment for bad wave paddling is a lot less drastic in Florida than in most other areas of the country. If you go over, the waves will usually push you to shore with little more than sand burns as your worst injury. The gently sloping beaches give the waves a fairly constant shape with dumping waves unusual.

When the wind conditions reach a certain level, whitecaps will form. This can happen on any non-sheltered body of water in the state. It's usually a good sign to go in closer to shore or paddle the lees.

Waterspouts/tornados and hurricanes/thunderstorms and lightning. These are the scary things you don't want to deal with if you have a choice. All occur in Florida at one time or another during the year but can be avoided with some reasonable planning.

Waterspouts are small tornadoes that occur over water. They can be seen as narrow dark "strings" descending to the water from the edges of black thunderheads and traveling along with the storm. They usually fall apart and reform from time to time and disappear forever once they hit land. With winds in small ones generally in the 50-knot-plus range, these are not nice things to get caught in. If you spot one nearby, track its path and paddle like hell in the opposite direction. Get to land and batten down if you can't outrun it. Since these usually occur out of those dark thunderstorm clouds, avoid storms and you'll avoid waterspouts.

Florida ranks 2nd nationally in the number of recorded tornadoes annually. Usually found around hurricanes and very violent thunderstorms during spring or fall fronts, these are usually not a problem for paddlers. Of course, when they occur over water, watch out. Waterspouts are columns of twisting water, much like tornadoes. Though waterspouts are not as fast or intense as tornadoes, they can certainly be damaging. They are most common in Florida during May through October.

Hurricanes can be a major problem for any unwary (that's another name for "stupid") paddler. You should have a minimum of 12 hours to get out of the way of a hurricane. Depending on size and location from shore, you can sense the wave changes as much as 36 hours ahead. Hurricanes are flighty beasts, never quite going where they should and showing up at the most inopportune times.

To impress upon you the wisdom of being far inland (try Missouri) when a big hurricane hits, let me share some personal information and stories. First, most hurricanes turn out to be just big rain and wind storms, causing very little damage except for a few miles around the eye. A few are major killers. Unfortunately, you can't always tell the difference in advance. I've sat through the edges of ten or fifteen hurricanes. I actually paddled in my little sheltered river when the winds were reaching 60 mph downriver, causing 1-1/2' to 2' waves. It wasn't supposed to be within 30 miles of me at the time.

In the 1950s, I lived in Daytona Beach and watched surf break over the top of sand dunes that have since been removed for the placement of a motel. Had the motel been there in the '50s, the waves would have been crashing into the middle of the second floor. I've also talked to reliable eyewitnesses who saw a two-by-four stuck through the middle of a palm tree after a bad hurricane in the 1940s. The projected storm surge in the Ft. Myers area is approximately 26' above normal tide lines. Hurricane Andrew, which hit South Florida in 1992, produced so many strange stories (grass sticking in concrete walls) that the truth is hard to believe.

Hurricanes are Mother Nature's way of releasing excess ocean heat. They are upwelling air currents around a spiral circulation that lifts huge quantities of moisture into rain clouds. I'd briefly considered giving a little information about wind directions and things like that but decided the only thing coastal paddlers in Florida need to know about hurricanes is to get out and go away until they do.

Thunderstorms and lightning are another natural phenomena you need to understand before you paddle in Florida. The central west coast gets more each year than anywhere in the U.S. (by some reports). If you paddle between April and November, you'll probably deal with one or more. In the summer you can hardly avoid them. Here's my best advice.

If you see dark clouds building before you get onto the water, don't go out until they leave. If you're on the water when the clouds come, try to get to shore if you can. If you can't, put on your skirt, raincoat and PFD and watch for the waves to build. Point into them and wait out the storm, keeping as low and balanced as possible. Unless you're in the path of a line of storms, singles will pass over in a few minutes. The most dangerous period is usually the beginning, with high winds, lightning, and rain. Once the front edge passes, the water is usually very calm with periods of lighter rain. I love paddling during this time on hot summer days.

In the first draft of this book, I wrote that I didn't know of any kayakers who had been struck by lightning. Unfortunately, my editor sent me a story from the *Sarasota Herald-Tribune* of July 17, 1994, describing a kayaker who was killed by lightning in Sarasota Bay, 150 yards from shore. The report states that the 24-year-old man was struck just before a thunderstorm passed overhead, before any rains appeared. He was paddling a whitewater boat and his aluminum-shafted paddle showed lightning entry and exit marks. This is the first reported lightning death of a kayaker to my knowledge. I hope it's the last.

Since we have only this one experience to work with, it's difficult to extrapolate hard and fast rules. The aluminum paddle may have been the key. Fiberglass and wooden paddles do not conduct electricity to any degree. Unfortunately, we just don't know. Rule one is to stay out of the water if it looks threatening during thunderstorm season. The rest of the rules are educated guesses.

If lightning starts striking all around you, do you head for the nearest shore or hunker down and wait it out? I'm not sure I know.

If your boat and paddle are non conducting, it's probably better to cover up and get as low in the water as you can. If you're close to shore, head in and stay low. Run the boat up into the marsh grass and wait it out. Stay away from tall trees or other tall objects. Seek better advice on this one than I can give.

2. Tides

In most Florida waters, knowing the tides is very important. We don't have any Bay of Fundy tides (25′), but the effects may be surprisingly similar because of the shallow, sloping coasts. We get the usual four tides a day, about six hours apart. Twice a year we get spring tides with very high highs and low lows. Even during these periods the tides rarely exceed 5′. However, 5′ vertically may be as much as 2 miles horizontally depending on beach slope. Check your local newspaper or buy a set of tide tables to take with you.

Low energy coasts/inland. Knowledge of tides is most important for the paddler along the Everglades, Ten Thousand Islands, Big Bend, and the inland systems. I can remember waking up one morning on a beach north of Steinhatchee in the Big Bend and looking out into the fog and seeing no water. We had come in during a nice high tide all the way to this great sandy beach and when we got up all we could see was mud. I've also tried to beat a falling tide just south of this area and got trapped in the middle of a mile and a half mud flat. I had to pull/paddle to an island near the previous night's campsite and sit out the next six hours until there was enough water.

You have to understand about mud in Florida. There's mud and then there's MUD. The low-energy coasts are covered with both varieties. Mud is when you only sink up to your upper calf. MUD is when you go over your knee. Paddling out of Flamingo in Everglades National Park one winter, we made a bad tide decision and were trapped near shore. I got out to begin pulling the boat and discovered that I was still going down when the MUD reached my crotch.

In most places along the Big Bend coast, the mud is just a nuisance that you learn to live with. If you plan to paddle at mid and high tides, you will hardly even notice it. If the tides fall wrong and you hit some zero or minus low tides, you'll normally have to pull your boat into or away from the shore. The only way you can avoid mud or MUD is to keep track of the tides.

Strong winds also affect the low tides in this area. Cold fronts in the winter have been known to thwart paddling plans that depend on accurate tide data. The water doesn't come back in like it should. We had to paddle in 6″ to 10″ of water for a whole day, more than a mile from shore because the waves were too high off shore and the tide wouldn't let us get inside. Five hours of that kind of paddling is not fun.

If you need to be somewhere along this coast at a specific time, you may have to leave a lot earlier than expected or alter your campsite to get around the tides. We missed an easy lunch pickup by two hours (from an hour and a half away) because we couldn't float the boats. The next night we camped on a spoil island near the channel so we could get out into deeper water without pulling our boats too far through the mud. The next morning we got into the channel with little trouble but discovered we had to go out of sight of land in the fog in order to find deep enough water. That's why you bring your compass. Actually, the water was clear enough that we just paddled the 18″ depth contour and a general heading until the tide came in far enough that we could see land again.

The worst a kayaker can face from not giving due care to the tides along these coasts is long, hard pulls through mud and over oyster bars. If you plan properly, you can avoid most of these difficulties. If you screw up, plan a few extra hours of work. We paddled by a stranded sailboat that had been stuck for a week after being blown inshore by a thunderstorm near Keaton Beach. The owner expected the tides to be high enough to float him off in another week or so. He walked to town through the shallow water and mud for groceries every few days and otherwise seemed content to wait it out. Kayakers should not have that kind of problem.

The tides in the intercoastal system are similar to the low-energy coasts and the mud is pretty much the same. My experience has been that you rarely have as many long pulls through the mud in the inland areas as you do on the Gulf or Florida Bay. However, the mud can have more trash in it and be more polluted with industrial waste, depending on where you decide to paddle.

High-energy coasts. The tides seem to be less important on the high-energy beaches because of the sandy shores. On a few beaches at bottom low tides (the Daytona Beach area is a good example), you might have some long sandy drags to make, as much as 100 yards. The waves will be different if the beach slopes change, but otherwise there is little worry for the kayaker unless the beach has suffered severe erosion and it disappears at high tide. The location and disturbances caused by sand bars can also change with the tides, so be on the lookout for these features. If you expect to leave and come back to a particular beach, look at the tide signs before you go so you can get a feel for what you may have to face when you get back. Seaweed lines, sharp erosion banks, and hard sand lines can all be fairly good indicators of high-tide locations. The tides will have an effect on some inlets. Rips, swirls, and choppy waves can result if tides and wind conditions are right. Be very careful around the more narrow inlets.

Keys. There are few tides in the Florida Keys that will have a major impact on the sea kayaker unless you get close to the mainland. Few, if any, of the islands have normal tidal changes that will stop a kayaker. Except for the usual mud walks and blocked passageways between some of the small islands, you shouldn't have much trouble if you're careful.

Weather Information. By far the best weather information is the up-to-date temperature and radar on your wireless internet connection. If you have that level of techno-goodies, enough battery power and cell coverage, by all means use it. If you're like the rest of us, a small NOAA weather radio works fairly well in most areas. It's always a good idea to take one along since local boaters are notoriously unreliable when it comes to sharing weather information (this may be changing since wireless connections have become more popular).

Summary

Florida has lots of weather. Learn your particular location's specifics, listen to the local NOAA weather station and watch weather radar. Treat bad weather with respect. If in doubt, don't.

Chapter 10

COASTAL CRITTERS FOR ENJOYMENT AND PAIN

Florida's coastal waters and lands are loaded with wonderful and awful critters. This chapter will give you a non-scientific kayaker's look at the fauna you may meet and what to do and not do about them.

1. Birds

Florida has a mess of birds. I'm a "birder" so I know what I say. More than 400 species can be seen with a lot of work over a substantial period of time. What you'll see depends on when and where you paddle. Look for tropicals like roseate spoonbills and reddish egrets in the south and ducks representing almost all North American eastern species in the north in winter. The shores will be dotted with egrets and herons and the ubiquitous double-crested cormorant is everywhere. Add gulls, brown and white pelicans, terns, and various shorebirds and there's a lot to keep you interested. Florida's population of bald eagles is second only to Alaska's and they're being seen more and more along the Gulf Coast.

I always bring my binoculars and bird book and keep them handy in the boat. Though you don't see a lot of variety while paddling, there's always something out there to check out. Once you hit shore, the variety picks up enormously, particularly if you're stopping at a spot with some habitat diversity like a river mouth or hardwood hammock. Spring and fall bring in migrants, and storms on either coast can produce some strangers from the Midwest or Caribbean. Fifty to sixty different species in a day would not be unusual for the ordinary kayaker, though Audubon Christmas bird counts can be well over 150. The hawk migrations along the northwest Florida beaches in the fall produce everything from peregrine falcons to flocks of the more common raptors.

Unfortunately, even though we have a lot of wading birds along the shore, almost 90 percent of historic levels in the south have disappeared because of habitat destruction, interruption of fresh water flow and overfishing. There's still plenty to see, but they aren't like they used to be.

2. Land Mammals

Land mammals are fairly common along Florida's coasts, though you probably won't see many. There are numerous kinds of beach mice and rats along with rabbits, nutria, mink, gray squirrels, skunks, raccoons, possums, foxes, deer, and feral hogs that move in and out of coastal areas. None are going to be very common during the daytime and only raccoons and skunks will intentionally visit your campsites at night. There may be an occasional black bear passing through in a few selected areas, but for the most part, these are too rare to cause any concern. One was picked up swimming 2 miles off the coast recently, but that's the first time I've ever heard of one in that situation. The National Wildlife Refuges will be the best places to explore for land mammals, particularly up the freshwater rivers and creeks.

The only common mammal you should expect to see is the ubiquitous armadillo. Since its invasion from the Southwest in the last 50 to 100 years, this armored land mammal has become quite common in the state. They are often seen wandering around coastal hammocks. There are a number of interesting facts about armadillos. They are harmless to humans, have very poor eyesight, eat mainly bugs, thrash about loudly in the bushes (day and night) and, when frightened, jump straight up in the air before running away (that's why there are so many "sail" armadillos on the roads). They have nasty digging claws that can scratch if you try to play with them. Don't sneak up on them while they wander on the beach, grab their tails and yank them quickly off the ground so your admiring buddies can take your picture with a squirming armadillo for the folks back in Kansas. If you hear loud noises in the bushes at night, you probably have an armadillo and not a bear or panther.

3. Marine Mammals

Florida doesn't have the marine mammals of the northern coasts. We don't have seals and sea lions nor do we have many whales. We do have a lot of porpoises, however, that can appear anywhere and make your whole day. We also have the 2,000-pound lovable sea slug called the West Indian manatee.

If you see a whale while paddling in Florida, you may be the first sea kayaker to do so that year (or ever). Pilot whales wash up on the Atlantic shore from time to time, and I saw a dead minke whale on a sandbar in the St. Marks River in the Big Bend ten years ago. The mouth of the St. Johns River in northeast Florida is the calving grounds for the right whale but I don't know any kayaker who's seen one. A pod of killer whales was sighted in the Gulf of Mexico 60 miles south of Panama City, but that's the closest they've come, to my knowledge. Forget about looking for whales while in Florida. You may stumble onto one, but the possibility is so rare in coastal waters that it's hardly worth mentioning.

Porpoises or bottlenose dolphins are very common. Sometimes you can get close to them and sometimes you can't. They're the ones who make that decision, not the paddler (as it should be). I always stop and watch for a while if they come by. The babies and yearlings seem more interested in you than the adults, but none seem to do more than take a look and go on about their business. Their fishing antics are always fun to watch if you're in the right place at the right time. I've seen one feeding on mullet in shallow water (18″ to 2′) by herding them in circles, charging into the school at full speed, doing a 180-degree turn and flipping the fish into the air and catching it in his/her mouth before hitting the water. The porpoise would repeat this four or five more times until it had enough. I think it was just showing off. However,

I saw the same behavior at about the same time the next year in the same place, and others have reported similar actions in Everglades National Park.

I've never felt threatened by porpoises. A few years ago I paddled up on a young pair near Lanark Village, east of Apalachicola. They were traveling the same direction I was but at a slightly slower speed. When I got within 10′, one of them turned its head, eyeballed me for a second, and both dove in unison with a great splash to the left, down to the bottom, turned 180 degrees, passed under the bow of the boat close enough to lift it a few inches, straightened out and continued on the same line as they started but at a much higher speed. They soon disappeared from view. The water was clear and only 6′ deep. It was exciting but not threatening. They're neat critters.

Florida is the last remaining U.S. habitat for the endangered West Indian manatee. There are approximately 2,000 left in the wild. In the summer you can run into one just about anywhere along the coastal waters if you're very lucky. The knowledge that one is near you can be very exciting, but their in-water habits are about as tension-producing as watching paint dry. They eat aquatic grasses and breath loudly through their noses as they surface.

Motorboats have been manatees' main enemies since the locals stopped eating them. They're too slow to get out of the way of the faster boats. That's why most have those ugly scars in the shape of whirling propellers all over their backs. Winter paddling near warm-water refuges such as Crystal River and the power plants in the Intercoastal Waterway can almost guarantee a sighting. Summer paddling around the mouth of the Suwannee River and its islands can also produce a few. Remember, manatees are an endangered species. Don't mess with them. Not only is it bad paddling etiquette to intentionally go near one, it's also considered harassment and you may wind up in jail or heavily fined.

4. Snakes

There are few snakes in Florida's coastal waters. Even fewer of these are poisonous. There are no sea snakes and the others do not prefer salt water. You may see an occasional rattlesnake or cottonmouth (water moccasin) near freshwater streams or ponds, but these will be quite rare along the salt coasts. Most sightings will occur paddling along the Intercoastal where freshwater ponds are common near the salt water. There are five or six Rattlesnake Islands named on these inland routes. I don't know if they got that name because they had lots of rattlesnakes there or because someone saw one and was surprised. I suggest you take the same precautions you would inland in Florida. Watch where you put your feet and hands. Step over logs with care. Learn what to do about snakebite. In the nine years I've paddled my kayak along Florida's coasts, I haven't seen a snake in salt water.

5. Alligators/Crocodiles

Once endangered because of overhunting, Florida's alligator population is growing and healthy. Unless they've been fed by humans, alligators pose no real danger to the kayaker. Even if hand fed, they probably aren't much of a problem. Florida's alligators are rarely aggressive except for females protecting eggs in nests. Nests in salt water are rare. Alligators do travel in salt water but prefer the freshwater systems. You'll most likely see a traveling snout near the entrances to rivers and salt creeks. I almost stepped on one while fishing once, but that was the only close call I've had. The gator didn't even move and I jumped into the boat and went elsewhere.

Crocodiles only occur in the area around Everglades National Park and the Upper Keys. They are reclusive and almost never seen by boaters. They are also not aggressive.

6. Oysters

Oysters are the most dangerous of the animals in Florida's coastal environment. There are more injuries from oysters than any other critter by far. Their razor-sharp shells do wonders to the bottoms of feet and boats alike. They tear your hands and have a way of making a trip a real problem if you don't look out for them and take the proper precautions. Once you "oysterize" your mental processes and dress appropriately, they move way down on the list of problem animals. The biggest problem I now have with oysters is that they are so good to eat and there are so few out of the many that can be eaten. They are too polluted to even chance unless you are in one of the few selected areas that are open for harvest.

7. Jellyfish, Stingrays, Sea Urchins, Sharks

This wide category of possible problems are generally at the low nuisance level unless you make some stupid mistakes or are taken by surprise.

Jellyfish are common throughout Florida but the East Coast variety has the worst sting. The Portuguese man-of-war is the worst of the worst. They blow in at certain times of the year and can give a very bad sting if you're swimming or pulling onto a beach unawares. Avoid the long tentacles.

Stingrays are a problem only if stepped on. They have a sharp barbed spear or spears on the tail and can stick it into you if you're dumb enough to step on them. The spear is barbed, very tough to pull out and can get infected easily. Shuffle along if you're walking on muddy bottom and they'll swim rapidly away. They don't want you to step on them. They will not attack. Be prepared; they are very common throughout most of the state.

Sea urchins are common in the Keys and can be found in lesser quantities as you travel north. The long-spine variety appear as purple flowery pincushions all over the reefs. They can be very painful if stepped on. The spines break off in your body and are hard to remove. If they become infected, seek immediate medical treatment. Though sea urchins can move along the bottom, they don't move fast and they don't move far. You avoid them by avoiding them. Look before you step and you won't have any problems.

Sharks may be a minor problem in some areas, but there are no reported shark attacks on kayakers in Florida. Major migrations occur along both coasts in the spring when they often feed in the surf or near shore. Surfers who hang their feet over their boards have been bitten. Deep channels in all areas of Florida may have sharks. I've never run into one, though I saw three caught off the beach in Everglades National Park in April. If you see a big shark who insists on staying around you, go the other way or get into shallow water.

8. Bugs, Bugs, Bugs

Florida would be a kayaker's paradise if it weren't for the bugs. I'd even camp in the summer if there were no bugs. Few will bother you while actively paddling in open salt water, but any interaction with shore can be a problem. All can be repelled for a period of time with the normal repellents and proper clothing. Unfortunately, when the populations are high, they can find places where repellents dare not go, and the whole trip becomes a disaster. That's why I camp only in winter. There still may be bugs, but they're a whole lot more manageable. The only sure antidote is a stiff breeze blowing on shore. The following list some of my favorites.

No-See-Ums. The sand gnat is my least favorite of all the bugs in salt water. In the spring, you can be attacked by great swarms as you land along the coast. These may be gray clouds of tiny, biting terrorists that move around like ill-defined ghosts or the normal thousands that move closer to the ground as the temperature cools off. In large quantities, they get into everything and the tickling in your nose and ears can be almost as annoying as their bites. The Avon bath oil, Skin So Soft, works well most of the time, but like other repellents can be overcome by numbers. Net hats and long sleeves help, but unless you sew up your buttonholes, they will find naked, untreated skin. Under these conditions, don't land, or if you have no choice, hit the beach running. No-see-ums can show up any time of the year the temperature is over 70 degrees but are most prevalent spring through fall. They usually go away at night when the mosquitoes come out.

Mosquitoes. Everyone knows about mosquitoes. We have a zillion varieties in Florida that fit practically every ecosystem. They range from good old possibly disease-carrying freshwater varieties to salt marsh mosquitoes that are usually small but are vicious biters. They come out when the no-see-ums leave. Mosquitoes can be found at all times of the year except during cold weather in the north. If you don't know by now how to protect yourself from mosquitoes, it won't do much good for me to tell you. Florida mosquitoes can compete with any in the world under the right conditions. In some parts of the state (the Everglades are a good example) there may be no mosquitoes one minute and you'll be totally covered in 5 to 10 seconds. Be prepared when the sun starts going down.

Horseflies. The pest of the salt flats in summer. They can be as big as hummingbirds but are usually slow enough to kill easily. The problems arise when you want to do something other than swat. Wear long things and hope for a breeze.

Dog Flies. These are biting flies that look like common houseflies. They tend to show up in late summer and fall but can show up in winter if the weather warms. They don't inject anti-coagulants so they don't raise welts, but their bite can sting. They have a nasty habit of finding your lee side and swarming. I can remember a time a few years ago near Steinhatchee when the dog flies came out in a warm December. They were buzzing around my face and trying to bite my arms when they seemed to disappear when a breeze came up. I remarked on their disappearance to my paddling companion, who pointed out I had a thousand attached to my back (waiting for the wind to die so they could find open skin). These seem to be more resistant to insect repellent than any of the others, but they are also slower biters and aren't around as long.

Yellow/Deer Flies. Without a doubt, the yellow fly is the most treacherous biting fly in Florida. It's like a horsefly, but a more rapid flyer, about a half inch long with a dark yellow/orange body. It is generally a freshwater critter, but it can be found on shore near salt water. It's the only living creature I would delight in tearing one wing off of and letting it dance around in circles until it dies. Yellow flies seem to come out when the blackberry blossoms show up in the spring and disappear or decline in numbers when the blackberry fruits have fallen, usually early to midsummer. They have a vicious bite that often leads to major swelling the first few times. They're so annoying because not only can they buzz in multiples around your body while searching for a tasty morsel, but they also land on you so lightly you can't feel them. By the time you feel them bite, it's too late to do anything. You've already received a good dose of anti-coagulant, so you can anticipate a lot of itching and swelling. If you see one land and try to kill it, the bugger usually flies off too fast, so you add insult to injury by needlessly smacking your body as well. If you want to kill them (and you will!!!), watch them land with their heads up. Don't swat them yet. When they put their head down to sup on your blood, swat quickly. Don't wait too long. They're almost impossible to kill in the heads up position, so don't even bother. Insect repellent will work on these if you cover and recover well. It won't keep them from buzzing, however.

Fire Ants. These ants are a variety imported from South America a number of years ago. They are small but vicious when disturbed. They live in sandy mounds that can be up to a foot or so high and are often found on the upper part of low-energy beaches around the state. They bite when disturbed either because you stepped on their nest or stayed in the way of their march to or from food. The "fire" in "fire ants" describes how the bite feels. If you get them on you, jump in the water as fast as you can and then brush them off. People with allergic reactions to insect bites should carry the appropriate medicine. If you're a basically inquisitive person with a low environmental ethic, you can stir a stick in the nest to watch them boil out. Stand clear and leave the area before they find you. Don't set up your tent on or near their nests. Most of the other ants on the beaches are easy to avoid and rarely give much trouble unless you're not very attentive.

9. Corals

In the southern part of the state, mainly the Keys, you will find some of the few living coral reefs in the continental U.S. Coral reefs are piles of living animals covering the hard, white limestone remains of earlier corals. The white coral rocks you buy in the shell stores are the skeletons of the dead corals. The live corals come in many shapes and sizes and contain ecosystems of remarkable diversity and beauty. They are protected throughout the state and should not be molested. In some places, patch reefs are close to shore and in others, a few miles offshore. During the right times of the year (mainly the summer), you can safely paddle out to some of the big reefs if you're willing to spend the time and effort. This is a trip only for the experienced and well-equipped paddler. The rest of you should look at the smaller inshore reefs.

Certain corals, particularly fire coral, can act much like poison ivy if they scratch unprotected skin. Buy an identification guide before you try the reefs. Swimming around coral reefs can be one of the most incredible experiences of your life; however, there are also dangers and problems you should be aware of before you venture too deep. Find a good book in the area to help you with them.

Summary

Florida has wonderful wildlife and bugs along its shores. Look for the former and protect yourself from the latter. Paddle in winter—you'll be happier.

Chapter 11

COASTAL VEGETATION OF NOTE

The coastal areas of Florida are covered with vegetation that's important both to the systems in which they exist and to the sea kayak user. Some are harmless to humans and some are not. Much has been damaged over the years by man's use and must be protected if the remaining ecosystems are to survive. This chapter is a quick run-through of some of the important examples.

1. Sea Grasses

As you paddle through glassy seas along the west coast or the inland waterway in the south, you will pass over numerous beds of sea grasses. These masses of vegetation form the basis for the estuarine food chains that are so important for recreational and commercial fisheries. They are harmless to humans but are usually not good walking areas because they trap sediments and are quite mushy. If you have to drag through grasses, keep to the clear areas as much as possible. You will find walking easier and you won't harm the grass.

Interspersed among the grasses, at various depths, are a whole host of other vegetable-like things such as sea fans and sponges that fit a similar ecological niche but are not as plentiful (some are actually animals). Don't pick, play with, spindle, or mutilate them. We like them where they are. Look for washups on the beach if you have to take some back with you. A note of warning: They all smell when drying so don't be surprised when they throw you off the plane in Atlanta on the way home.

Motorboats do the most damage to these grasses in the shallow waters, while pollution in the form of increased turbidity takes care of the rest. There is also an industry starting that collects unusual specimens for the tourist trade, which could be a bad problem in the future. Remember, as a kayaker, don't even leave footprints if you can help it. Leave nothing but wakes as you pass.

2. Marsh Grasses

The marsh grasses are those longer-stemmed grasses that are out of the water during some part of the day and prefer damp to wet. They are horrible to walk through and should be looked at and bypassed. The amount of muck under them can be bottomless to the luckless person who has no choice but to cross them. One common variety is called "needlegrass" because of the sharp points at the tip. These grasses can be a real bad problem after major storms when they become buried by sand. As 4' grasses, they maintain a lot of flexibility and will bend as they stick you. When only a few inches stick out of the ground, they can inflict a very painful puncture wound. Check the sand before you move in. We camped on a new beach after a hurricane and didn't look. Everything had holes in it by the time we left, including ankles and shins.

The marsh grasses are important parts of the coastal ecosystem, where they are the first line of defense against shore erosion in low-energy areas and provide good habitat for juvenile fish during high tides. They also serve as cover for numerous nesting birds like rails and wrens as well as play a part in filtering runoff from the land. They are most prevalent in the northern part of the state where mangroves won't grow. They provide some of Florida's most spectacular vistas as they stretch for miles along the coast, dotted occasionally with coastal hammocks.

3. Mangroves

The appearance of mangroves is the first sign of the shift from the temperate north to the tropical south. They start showing up in the Daytona Beach area on the east coast and the Cedar Key area on the west. The further south you go, the more common they get. By the time you get to the southern third of the state, the mangrove forests have replaced the marsh grass systems as the major coastal land/water interface. They serve similar ecological functions.

For the kayaker, mangroves mean a lot more trouble. Though walking through marsh grasses is difficult, whether pulling or not pulling a kayak, walking though mangroves with a kayak is impossible and without one is difficult at best. Since one of the ecosystem functions of the mangrove plant is to drop a lot of leaves and trap them among its roots to provide food and protection for sea life, the areas around the roots are usually unconsolidated soils (muck)—deep muck. To move through mangroves that do not have sufficient water channels to float your boat, you mostly have to climb the roots as you stumble through. This works better in the bigger trees that are further back from the coast but is almost impossible in the smaller plants near the water. Most of the plants near the water are covered with barnacles and small oysters that will rip your skin off. I generally consider mangroves impenetrable and leave them alone. (They also harbor a lot of mosquitoes from the coastal breezes. Picture yourself stumbling over roots, mud up to mid-thigh, sliced and bleeding from barnacles, sweating in 100-degree temperatures, and being surrounded by the worst biting mosquitoes in the world. Sounds like a vacation, right?)

4. Sea Oats and Other Dune Vegetation

Sea oats and other vegetation that grows on sand dunes are very important for the stability of the dune and the beach system it supports. If the sea oats and other vegetation is removed, the dune goes, and soon the beach will follow. Dunes have a lot of other valuable purposes as well. Try not to dig holes in, walk gullies in, or otherwise damage dunes or their vegetation. As kids growing up in Daytona Beach in the 40s and 50s, we used to do all three of those in our youthful ignorance. We tunneled into the dunes for "secret hideouts," walked through on the same paths until they became deep gullies, and pulled up the sea oats to throw at each other like spears. There are few sand dunes left in Daytona Beach and the beaches are rapidly eroding, as they are throughout the state. I probably wasn't totally responsible, but I carry around my share of the guilt. Leave the dunes alone and you won't have this terrible burden to carry for the rest of your life.

5. Dangerous Plants

There are a number of plants along the coast of Florida that can cause you harm if you're not careful. Most are pretty obvious, but a few can sneak up on you. The following are the most common, though others exist in the subtropical areas.

Prickly pear cactus. These are the flat-eared cactus with long spines that are quite prevalent throughout Florida. They tend to be more numerous along the low-energy shores and in the back dunes of the high-energy beaches. The spines are stiff and painful, like most cacti. In the Big Bend area they can grow in large colonies close to the shore. If you see the large plants in the vicinity, look for the smaller ones under the low bushes as well. Their fruit is edible as described below.

Spoil island thornys. The spoil islands dredged up near channels have an amazing amount of thorny vegetation on them that you will rarely see anyplace else. I presume the rapid drainage of the pumped up dirt and low nutrient retention allow only the hardiest vegetation to survive the first ten or twenty years. Though these islands are usually good for camping because of smooth sandy places and some benign vegetation like cedar trees and cabbage palms, they can be very rough in spots.

Stinging nettles. Stinging nettles occur on and around the dune systems of the east coast as well as in sandy open spaces just about anywhere. They are friendly little low green bushes (3″ to 24″) with small white single flowers that grow almost in isolation from their near neighbors. The leaves look "furry" upon close inspection. These little "furry" hairs are actually small hypodermic needles with a bulb of formic acid at the plant end. When you grasp them, they inject small quantities of acid into your flesh, causing great itching. They're nasty little buggers for the unwary and barefoot. They feel much like mild ant bites.

Sandspurs. Sandspurs stick to you when you brush against them. They are the most common cause of mild pain to barefoot paddlers in Florida. Some beach areas are covered with them. Avoid these. When you get one in you (and you will if you paddle for any time around Florida), and you don't have tweezers handy, wet your fingers before you pull them out. This will keep them from sticking in your hand after you pull them out of your foot. Though they rarely grow right next to the water on most beaches, a few of the stickers always seem to be buried in the sand in areas where they're common. You don't know they're there until they stick in your foot. The safe practice is to always wear your footgear until you're satisfied the sand is clean.

Spanish bayonets. These plants are usually fairly large (3' to 6'), green leafy stalks in the yucca family. They're found on a number of low-energy beaches and back of the dune systems on the high-energy beaches. The ends of each of the leaves that radiate out from a center stalk is a 2″ to 3″ spike that can really stab you if you're not careful. They often form an impenetrable barrier on some beaches. Numerous birds nest in these plants in the spring, if isolated enough, because of the protection they give from marauding raccoons and other critters.

6. Edibles

There are a number of edible plants along the coasts of Florida, but I wouldn't depend on any for sustenance unless you're really hungry. (Did you ever stop to think that most wild plants that are good tasting have already been cultivated?) Most of the vegetation needs protection, so I'm only mentioning two plants whose picking won't do much harm if selectively taken. Taste one or two to say you have and leave the rest for someone else. I'm not a real connoisseur of freeze-dried food, but I have found that wild vegetables rank slightly below it for taste pleasure. Keep that in mind before you get greedy.

Prickly pear fruit. When the fruit of the prickly pear turns deep purple and comes off the plant with an easy twist, they're ripe and almost good. The inside is a blood purple filled with jelly and seeds. The outside is smooth except for a number of clumps of hairy fibers. Beware! These hairy fibers are insidious painmakers. If you want to eat one of these fruits, wear gloves, cut off the hairy clumps with a sharp knife or avoid them completely. When clean enough, cut the fruit in half and squeeze the jelly into your mouth. They taste sort of sweet and fruity. Throw away the rind and spit out the pits. Frankly, they're hardly worth the effort except to try. I played hero with these on one trip by cutting them for people and squeezing them into their mouths. Unfortunately, I was not as careful with the hairy clumps as I should have been, and my former friend complained bitterly until I used the tweezers from my Swiss Army knife to pull out the almost invisible hairs from his lips.

Stinging nettle roots. The light brown root bulbs of this plant are also relatively reasonable to eat. Dig under the plant, below the last line of injectors, and pull out the root. Wash the root carefully and eat it raw. Don't even think of eating any other part of the plant! The root tastes "nutty" and about 4,000 will make dinner (with what untold consequences afterward I do not know). I developed a taste for these as a kid growing up on the beach, probably as a way to get back at the plant for the many times I was stung.

Summary

The Florida coastline is blessed with much vegetation that is important in maintaining the aquatic and beach ecosystems. Leave it alone if you can.

Chapter 12

EARLY COASTAL HISTORY

Florida has a long prehistory and history that's reflected in its coastal growth patterns. Because Florida was mostly water before the massive drainage projects of the late 19th and 20th centuries, much of its early exploration and settlement was along the coast. Today you'll find a great deal of Florida's history and prehistory open to you as you travel its 8,000 miles of shoreline.

The coastal paddler will often come across Native American and early historical sites, including a few well-placed forts. Understanding a little about these areas can add pleasure to any paddling experience, since you're traveling about the same speed they were and are seeing some of the same views. This will be a short chapter because many of you probably don't care about history and the rest of you want more than I'm willing to write. So, if you're interested, find a good book on the subject for the area you intend to paddle. If you don't care, skip this chapter.

A note about stealing native artifacts along the coast: The projectile points, pottery, and other artifacts you find along the coast belong to the state or the private landowners on whose property they are found. Don't take any with you. Once these artifacts are removed from the area, they lose all significance because they become unconnected to their past. Pick them up, look at them, photograph them if you want, and put them back where you found them.

I don't know if I care about "political correctness" but I am sensitive to the problems of those individuals who lived here before we stole their land. (Actually, they didn't understand the concept of "ownership" as it applied to land, considering their possession more a stewardship or trust than one of ownership, so stealing is a little harsh as applied here.) However, since my undergraduate major was in archeology at the University of Florida, and since I spent many days surveying and digging into old habitation and kill sites, and since I developed a lot of respect for anyone who could live in such a bug-infested, hot, muggy place without screens or air conditioning, I have decided to be as politically correct as I can when referring to our previous indigenous inhabitants while still retaining some flow. If you don't like the references, stop here and go to another chapter.

1. Prehistoric

PALEO PERIOD

The earliest Floridians were probably mammoth/mastodon hunters who moved from the Northwest on one of the migratory waves that came over from Siberia across the Alaskan ice bridge about 12,000 to 20,000 years ago. Unfortunately for you artifact hunters, most of the coastal living or hunting sites for these early people are underwater somewhere off the coast. It's generally accepted that 12,000 years ago, the water levels were 200 to 300 feet lower than today's levels because of the ice-age accumulations in the polar ice caps. The people who lived or hunted along the coast then had a very different shoreline than we have today. Their beach campsites may be as much as 20 to 50 miles off the present coast.

The best examples of artifacts from these early cultures are found today up the river systems that flow into the Gulf of Mexico, the Suwannee River being the best example. In the early '60s, archeologists discovered spear points in conjunction with mastodon bones at the confluence of the Suwannee, Sante Fe, and Ichetuckenee rivers. Projectile points of the same type have been found in the St. Marks, Econfina, and Peace rivers. It's theorized that the big mammal hunters drove their prey into the boggy edges of the rivers for easier killing.

ARCHAIC PERIOD

The first native Americans whose sites we find along today's coast came in around 6,000 to 8,000 years ago. They were hunters and gatherers with little, if any, agriculture. They didn't make pottery nor did they have bows and arrows. They did use flint and lots of shell tools constructed from conch or other plentiful hard-skinned sea life.

The coastal sites include small shell middens (garbage dumps) to large ceremonial mounds and a number in between. Most of the sites were on slightly higher land close to the coast that they made higher by depositing whatever they finished eating there. They probably used most of these sites for food gathering and temporary shelter off and on during the year, since fresh water would have been sparse without a lot of work. Practically every piece of land on the low-energy coasts that stays above the highest tides was used by Native Americans. These same areas were used by the early settlers as well as present-day coastal paddlers and fishermen.

FORMATIVE PERIOD

Pottery and agriculture was introduced into the state around 2,000 to 4,000 b.c. Pot shards of various types can be seen on many of the beaches on the west coast, indicating a long period of habitation for most of the higher land. Though few areas close to the coast were suitable for agriculture, you can bet that those places where crops could be grown were used. Reports from the Crystal River mounds area show strong agriculture use into historic times.

Reports of Indians using the coastal routes for transporting goods and food are common. Trade goods from as far north as the central Mississippi Valley have been found in southern Florida, and shells from the Gulf are found in mounds throughout the Mississippi. Native paddlers were pressed into service during the early Spanish days to transport grain from the Spanish missions in the Tallahassee area up the Suwannee River for transport by oxcart to St. Augustine.

The early explorers told many tales of the fierce Indians who inhabited Florida's shores. These included stories of cannibals in the Keys and peaceful farmers in the Panhandle. Since most, if not all, were wiped out by our ancestors, we'll have to rely on the historic records for our information. The Native Americans who now inhabit Florida came mostly from Georgia and Alabama during the late 1700s and early 1800s after the previous inhabitants died from the white man's diseases or bullets.

The Indian sites along the coast of Florida are part of the few remaining indications of the life and times of these people. If you don't care for them when you come ashore, they'll be destroyed, and this valuable history will be lost to all of us. Feel free to sleep where they slept, eat where they ate, but turn no dirt and take no souvenirs except with your cameras.

2. Historic

The Europeans started supplanting the Native Americans around 1513 a.d. when Ponce de León first arrived, reportedly looking for the fountain of youth. Florida was probably discovered much earlier by slave traders who raided the Indian villages along the coast but kept no records, for obvious reasons.

There are numerous tales of Ponce de León's travels and a number of places that claim to be that marvelous fountain. So far, none of the claims of magic powers have been substantiated by scientific experiments published in juried publications. When paddling on a cool winter morning, with just a hint of fog on the water, I certainly feel a lot younger. Maybe science just hasn't caught up yet.

Ponce de León was the governor of Puerto Rico when he sailed in an attempt to colonize Bimini. Due to poor navigation, he missed the island and ended up around the future St. Augustine on the northwest coast of Florida. From there he traveled around the state, probably to the Charlotte Harbor area on the west coast, and returned to Puerto Rico. He came back to that same area in 1531 and tried to establish a colony. The existing inhabitants were not overly thrilled about bearded white guys taking over their land, so they ran them off after killing a few for good measure. De León was wounded and later died in Havana.

With the death of Ponce de León, Spain sent other explorers to find gold as they had done in Mexico. First Pánfilo de Narváez then Hernando de Soto came to make their own and Spain's fortune. Neither succeeded for a number of reasons, mainly lack of gold. After these and a few other failures, the Spanish decided to change their methods and colonize rather than use smash and burn exploitation (is there a difference?). They claimed sovereignty over the state except for a small French colony near the Jacksonville area which was destroyed in 1565.

At around the same time, Pedro Menéndez de Avilés successfully established the first permanent colony within the state at St. Augustine. Florida was ruled by Spain until 1763, when it was traded to the British for Cuba. The British had captured that island paradise at the end of the French and Indian Wars.

The British established a network of trading communities around Florida to exploit Indian labor and goods from the interior of the southern Gulf coast. Many of the businesses thrived until the Revolutionary War erupted and the British Crown had trouble defending areas this far away from the main action.

Taking advantage of this distraction, Spain, who had joined the war against England at the urging of the French, successfully attacked West Florida in the Pensacola area and occupied the area in 1781.

In 1783 Spain officially got Florida back from the British as part of the Treaty of Paris, which ended the American Revolutionary War. They unsuccessfully attempted to follow the British in establishing a plantation and trading base for the state. Because of Spain's expansion in Central and South America, they couldn't find enough interested colonists. After the Revolutionary War, a number of American settlers took up residence in remote locations to avoid Spanish detection and control. The Seminole Indians moved (or were chased) into Florida about this time and created a very unsettled situation.

Eventually Spain got tired of the hassle and gave up. In 1819, Florida became a colony of the United States. It achieved formal statehood in 1845.

During these historic times, numerous forts were built along the coast to protect shipping and settlements. Every major harbor entrance (and a few minor ones) from Pensacola to Fernandina Beach had some form of military installation. Modern-day towns such as Ft. Lauderdale and Ft. Myers were old fort sites, retaining the same names but with no remaining visible evidence.

There are, however, a few of the old structures still standing that are fun to paddle around. The best-preserved and oldest is the Castillo de San Marco in St. Augustine, now a federal historic monument. All of the old battlements are still in place and it makes a very impressive sight from the water. For you history buffs, it's not hard to imagine the battles that took place there.

The remains of another fort can be seen at the confluence of the St. Marks and Wakulla rivers south of Tallahassee. Only the bulwarks of Apalachee de San Marco remain, but this state historic site is interesting and there are some funky eating places nearby, along with the state's first rail-to-trail bike path.

For a little newer fort, try Fort Clinch at Fernandina Beach, which was used extensively during the Civil War. It's well-preserved with a lot of water access. You could also visit Fort Pickens at the Pensacola harbor entrance. It's part of the Gulf Island National Seashore that extends along the Alabama Gulf coast.

3. Modern

Modern Florida came into its own after the land booms and busts of the 1920s and 30s. Waves of people poured in for the sand and sun and low taxes, up to present day. This includes many from Latin countries, beset by war and famine. Even today we're getting more than 800 new residents a day. Since more than 80% of these migrants choose to live near the coast, true coastal wilderness adventures are rare.

All of the more sheltered waters of the state have been occupied by the various waves of migration. From Pensacola to Tampa Bay to Ft. Myers to Miami to Daytona Beach to Jacksonville, the bays have been surrounded by tall condominiums and dirty ports. How they got that way is not very important. Maybe we'll get a couple of good hurricanes and change the landscapes a little, but that's only wishful thinking.

Modern Florida history is little different from the history of the rest of this country in that the rush for the green dollar destroyed much of the natural green foliage and white sand that was the reason for the flowing of the dollars in the first place. It's a depressing story of well-meaning people, without a lot of knowledge, destroying much of natural Florida and refusing to stop when the knowledge was gained because the greed was just too strong. There's still a lot of what's beautiful out there for the sea kayaker; just look away from the shore when you need to.

Summary

This chapter was created to give a brief idea of what the history buff might find as he or she travels along the coast. It's mostly a depressing mix of warfare, cruelty, and greed. Have a happy paddle.

Chapter 13

OVERNIGHT PADDLING TRIPS

There are numerous opportunities for extended trips around Florida, including a full circumnavigation. However, there are only two areas that will give you a chance to experience Florida as it was before big growth occurred. The first area is the Everglades, mostly within Everglades National Park, where wilderness subtropical Florida still exists with only few changes caused by human occupation. The second area is the Big Bend coast, dotted with small, traditional fishing villages in transition to second home getaways but where most of the coast is still unspoiled.

These are very different areas, each providing the paddler with a view of Florida that can't be seen any other way. The following two chapters will discuss these areas in detail. The rest of this chapter will be devoted to trip planning and the other areas that may be available to you for overnight camping if you pass up the two recommended areas.

1. Trip Planning

Planning an overnight is either a terrible mess or a lot of fun, depending on your psychological needs and whether those needs meld with those of your paddling partners. "Balance" is the key word. Balance the weight in your boats and balance your partners.

A group of seven anal-retentive control freaks will have a lot of trouble. About the same as seven fuzzy-headed "everything's cool" dopeheads. However, if you have about half of each (let the extra one be a control freak—personal preference) and can reasonably cooperate, the planning should be just another part of a good experience.

Everyone has a different way of dealing with the initial planning, but I usually start out with how many days I want to stay out or where I want to go. If I know both, and they aren't mutually exclusive, the location and time are settled and the easy work begins. If they are, the next balancing process begins. Find a different place or shorten or lengthen the time of the trip. The only advice I have that seems to fit is: Go shorter rather than longer distances each day and try to find a place to put in that will minimize car travel. I hate to ride in a car for many hours, put in late and paddle until dark the first day. Yuck!

Before proceeding further, I have an important confession to make. When it comes to paddling long distances, I'm a first-class wimp. I usually plan my trips looking at books about long-distance travelers and then pare them down as the dates get closer. My ideal is a paddle of 10 to 12 miles per day, which I call "medium to easy." I expect it to take about five hours from launch to take out, including lunch stops and sightseeing. This allows me to get up around 7 a.m., get on the water by 9 a.m. and get into camp around 2 p.m. to 3 p.m., depending on the amount of sightseeing. Since dark is around 5:30 to 6:00 p.m. in the winter, this gives me plenty of time to set up camp, fish a little, and relax. With head winds, it's a little slower and with tail winds, faster.

I read with awe about the Inside Passage paddlers who average 25 miles a day from Juneau to Seattle. I've paddled 25 miles in a day and was not very happy during or after. I know I can do it, but I don't want to unless I have to. If your object is to paddle as fast as you can to get from place to place, I'm not writing for you. Just pick out some free water and go to it. If you want to see a little of saltwater Florida, read on.

All of the areas in Florida can be safely paddled by the complete novice with a little tutoring, practice, and common sense (weather conditions permitting) as long as he/she is a competent swimmer. The only exception may be the high-energy east coast. I do not recommend that novices (or experts for that matter) take off alone. Novices going on any extended trips on the water should go with someone who has on-water experience in the area or has substantial sea kayaking and camping experience generally.

My experience with novices in Florida (and other places as well) has taught me that the modern sea kayak does not require extensive practice for safe handling under benign weather and water conditions. Since Florida has mostly benign conditions, it is generally safe for novices. There are no sharp cliffs or headlands that make landing difficult. There is little surf that can't be avoided with proper planning and practically no rocks to crash into. There are few wild currents (stabilized inlets excepted) or whirlpools to drown you. The weather is generally predictable and weather information is available and accurate within 12 to 24 hours. If you go over, the water is warm, or not so cold that you can't get to shore before hypothermia sets in, or shallow enough to turn the boats over and dump out the water. So far, we have not recorded any shark attacks on kayakers. Most of the dangers you will face could result in "discomfort," but the chances of dying in these waters is so slight that you would have to be very, very unlucky for that to happen. So unlucky that it probably wouldn't matter if you were an expert or not.

Just so you'll know, the greatest dangers come not from the paddling or water conditions, but from general stupidity. Lack of fresh water is the main life-threatening problem. Carry enough in safe containers. Other possibilities include sunstroke, being struck by lightning, bitten to death by insects, eaten by sharks, alligators or crocodiles when you swim, dying of heart attacks, drowning, etc. I have not heard of any sea kayaking deaths in Florida to date except one recent lightning strike, so none of these events must be very common. General common sense will see you through just fine.

Regardless of how safe Florida can be for novices, I would always advise taking at least one experienced paddler and camper wherever you go. There are places (and weather conditions), however, that may look okay on paper or start out okay for novices and then turn bad if you don't avoid them or pre-plan around them. Crossings from islands over deep water, trips to offshore reefs, any northeast coastal trip, and some outside trips along the Panhandle beaches are among the most obvious that come to mind. Don't take novices on trips like this unless they have been well schooled (then they probably aren't real novices).

I've taken novices on practically every camping trip I've done in Florida and the trips have all turned out okay, despite one or two scares. With careful planning, novices should do just fine with an experienced hand along.

Use the information in this and the following chapters to work out the location and distance you plan to paddle. Pick out your put-in, take-out and overnight camping spots before you leave, to the greatest extent you can. Create a food list by calculating the number of meals and adding an extra meal or two for safety. You may put in after breakfast and take out after lunch, or plan to eat in a restaurant, etc., so multiplying the number of days by three won't usually work. Do a shopping list from the meal planner and check it off as you acquire food.

Do the food list and camping list at least a week before you leave (if this is your first trip in a while), or the night before if you've done this before and don't care that you may not find the food you want at the local convenience store. (See Appendix # 4.) Remember, the local store usually doesn't stock pitas or bagels and that little butane canister.

Check in often with your paddling partners to encourage their participation and keep them from wimping out on you. My first "expedition" had ten paddlers with two substitutes. I talked to each one every few days. (A later one had three paddlers because I announced where and when I was going and told everyone to sign on or not as they desired and didn't follow up.) This is particularly important if you're planning joint food or double kayaks. I always try not to plan joint food if there are more than three people going. In the larger groups, people can pair off and share with the others if they want. This usually makes for some exciting (and strange) meals.

Kayak livery can be simple or an awful pain. The simplest is to put in and take out at the same location. If that doesn't work, do a car swap with paddlers, friends, or relatives. Spouses are usually good for one of these a year. If you have the money, there are almost always canoe liveries somewhere nearby in Florida who will deliver and/or pick you up. The price will depend on the number in the party and distance of travel. Call your local canoe or outdoor shop for the latest information. Prices start around $50 and go up from there for any long distances. Arrange these as far ahead as you can to make sure whoever does it will be available. Look at the partial list of liveries in Appendix # 5.

2. Intercoastal Waterways

There are a lot of miles of Intercoastal Waterway within the state that are suitable for overnights. These are federally designated and maintained waterways for big boats to come down from New York or over from Houston. The long, straight channel along the east coast, just shoreward of the coastal ridge, is the most heavily traveled. Much of the northern part is "relatively" undeveloped and a pleasant place to spend a few days. Because the waters have been dredged (continuously) and the boat traffic is high, the waters are rarely clear and the banks are subject to substantial wake actions. However, the Intercoastal may be a good access path to many less traveled waterways.

The southern part of the Intercoastal on the east coast is mainly urban with a few miles of natural shoreline left. It's also important to remember to watch out for the large boats that use these waterways. They are often big and fast and can run up on you very quickly. Look for the sections that have state or county parks located at reasonable distances.

The intercoastal waterways on the west coast are more diverse, though still heavily traveled. Long-distance paddlers who want to avoid the Keys can cut across the state at Fort Myers through Lake Okeechobee and out into the Intercoastal on the other side (or vice versa). Like all inland lakes in Florida, Okeechobee is shallow and very rough during high winds. If you decide to go this way, plan an extra few days to circumnavigate the lake rather than going across the middle. If you ask at the right time, maybe some nice power boat will ferry you across.

I've paddled a number of areas of the intercoastal system but have not camped along them. I found them generally dirty, unpredictable, and not conducive to contemplation of the "meaning of life" as you leisurely paddle along. This may mean nothing to you if your usual paddling water is the lower Hudson River, but for those of us who like the less spoiled Big Bend area for winter and Alaska for summer, it means a lot.

As you might be able to tell, I'm not a fan of the intercoastal waterways so I don't spend much time on them in this book. However, people who live near them may have a different opinion, so you should inquire locally about good overnights. Sometimes you have no choice. They are water, and they do let you paddle on them, so when there is no other good alternative, enjoy!

3. Coastal Rivers

Many rivers in the state that empty into salt water would make great combination trips. The classic trip is the Suwannee River. It's almost 200 miles of mostly undeveloped river that comes out at the Gulf of Mexico at the town of Suwannee. Depending on water levels, moderate to easy river trips are usually 15-plus miles per day (downriver). There are two good publications for kayakers and canoers of Florida rivers (*A Canoeing and Kayaking Guide to the Streams of North Florida*, by Elizabeth Carter, and *A Canoeing and Kayaking Guide to the Streams of Central and Southern Florida*, by Lou Glaros).

A series of nice small rivers empty into the Gulf of Mexico in the Panhandle and Big Bend area about every 10 miles. They're all pleasant for side trips except the Fenholloway, which has been classed as Florida's only industrial river because much of its flow comes from a paper mill. It's dark and smelly. Others like the Chassahowitzka Homosassa, Crystal, Econfina, Aucilla, St. Marks, and Ochlockonee rivers give the paddler a nice break from the salt water. Expect a reasonable current against you and various water clarities from crystal clear to dark tannins. The temperatures are usually considered cool in the summer and warm in the winter (60 to 75 degrees).

These rivers are the larger ones you'll see marked on the road maps; however, there are numerous "salt creeks" and small streams that enter the Gulf, almost every few miles. All of them hold some attraction for exploring. They're also very useful for getting lost. If you decide to spend time "up the creeks," bring a compass or put markers at the bends. These streams have a nasty way of winding and turning back on themselves with only the marsh grasses to keep you company. I don't know about you, but I can't tell one stalk of juncus or spartina from another at water level.

Summary

The two best areas of the state for long trips in relatively natural settings are the Everglades National Park and the Big Bend Gulf Coast. Both areas present interesting and unique opportunities for the salt water paddler, but don't overlook the many other saltwater areas and coastal rivers if you can't make it to these areas.

Chapter 14

EVERGLADES NATIONAL PARK

Most out-of-staters, when they think of Florida paddling, think about going to the Everglades. It's the most highly publicized kayaking area of the state and may be the only one many of you have heard of (before reading this book, of course). This most endangered national park, called by its many protectors the "River of Grass," is a multi-faceted water system that will provide a variety of paddling experiences. There are numerous freshwater as well as saltwater opportunities. Since this is a book about sea kayaking, you can guess the ones I'm going to write about. (See Illustration 14-1. Everglades National Park.)

Before getting to the exciting facts about Everglades saltwater paddling, let me relate some personal facts and observations. I was 49 years old before I set foot in Everglades National Park. Since I'm a Florida native, and this was the only national park in Florida for most of those years, you might wonder why an outdoor person such as myself chose not to visit the state's one national park. The answer is very simple. I hate hot, muggy, buggy areas and never had the opportunity to camp or paddle the outside islands.

I've now taken three paddling trips in the park in the last ten years, and I still don't like hot, buggy places. I have, however, learned to appreciate certain aspects of the park, the essence of which I'll try to convey to you in this chapter. Like any other paddling trip in the world, your personal wants, desires, needs, and preconceptions will dictate your level of enjoyment, so who am to judge? The people who live in South Florida and paddle here really like this type of paddling. The jury is still out for me.

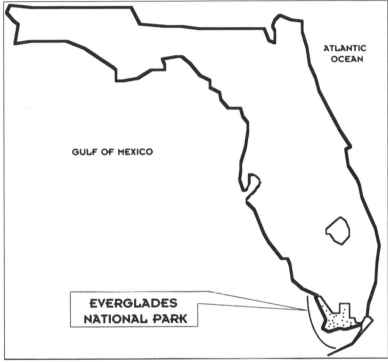

Illustration # 14-1. Everglades National Park

1. Trip Planning

There are a number of different types of saltwater trips you can make in the park, but there are only two land entrances: Flamingo in the south and Everglades City on the west side. Flamingo gives you direct access to Florida Bay, and Everglades opens up the Ten Thousand Islands. Both places have limited food, camping, and motel accommodations, but your real provisioning should be done before you arrive, unless you like convenience store shopping.

    If you feel that place names indicate your future, this may not be the best paddling area for you. With names like Shark River,

Lostmans Key, Graveyard Creek, Alligator Cove, and Sandfly Island, you might better stay home.

The complete outside paddling trip from Flamingo to Everglades City is around 85 miles or eight days of moderate to easy paddling. Whether you decide to paddle out of one area and come back to where you started or paddle the whole length of the park depends on your time constraints as well as weather conditions. Be sure to get the latest version of campsite information and maps from the park rangers before you go.

My suggestion is if you can afford the time, and have the means, you should use some livery system for a drop off at one end or the other and paddle the whole park. My reason for this is that not only will you have a nice paddle, but you have a better chance of going with the prevailing winds. Two of my trips would have been much better if I had read this book first and taken my own advice. More on that later.

If you can't do the long trip, and you're paddling in the winter (as anybody but a complete fool would do in this area), I'd do a circle route out of Everglades City or Chokoloskee and return to the same place. This will give you the best opportunities to take advantage of the winds. If the wind is too high outside, you can go inside, or if the bugs are too bad inside, you can stay out. There's a great deal more protection from the easterlies and southeasterlies on the west coast than on the south coast. You'll also have more flexibility if cold fronts are moving through.

The paddling in Florida Bay to the south is more challenging. There are longer crossings, more problems with prevailing easterlies, and a general feeling of openness that's good or bad depending on your point of view. It's also closer to Miami.

For those of you who want to do a one-way paddle, plan extra time for the car trips. It's around 130 miles from Everglades City to Flamingo by road through much of suburban Miami-Dade County. That's six to eight hours, depending on traffic. I know folks who've done it, but it's not my idea of fun.

2. Permits and Park Information

Before you paddle anywhere in the park, you must check in with the rangers for camping permits and let them know where you intend to stay. Depending on the number of parties out, certain camping spots can be closed. The outside is generally less crowded because they're almost all beach camping sites with more room and the canoes don't venture out as often. File a trip plan with someone at home as well so they can send out the planes when you don't show up. There's no charge for the permit.

The park will send you a nice brochure on paddling and camping and a pretty map with illustrations. See Appendix 6 for simplified campsite information. The maps sent by the park and the ones you see in this book are not meant for navigation. For that you need to buy those outrageously expensive waterproofed nautical charts that you can hang on your wall when you get home. Most marinas and sporting goods stores in South Florida have them. So does the marina at Flamingo. There's no way to read a tide table without one, so pony up unless you read water color very well.

3. Food and Gear

The park will send you a set of general maps and planning documents for your trip. The following is a summary of their recommendations and a few of my own.

Drinking water is the most important item for this trip. Bring enough water and food for your whole trip plus a day for safety. The park suggests a gallon of water a day per person. We carried three or four bottles of Gatorade-type drink and liked it a lot. If the weather's cool, you can get away with fewer liquids, but I wouldn't advise it.

Bring good bug spray. If the winds are up or temperatures are down, the bugs are usually minimal during the winter months (December through March). However, they get bad at any time if these are reversed. Mosquitoes, no-see-ums, and horseflies the size of hummingbirds can blossom in profusion when the winds die and the sun starts sinking. The park's "Backcountry Trip Planner" brochure should give you the best understanding of the situation. In discussing where to get your permit, the following sentence is inserted: "Insect conditions are so severe during summer months that backcountry use is minimal and permit writing desks may not be staffed." And you thought rangers were tough. 'Nuff said!

If you're going to paddle the outside of the park, expect to camp on sandy beaches and be prepared for high winds. You may be faced with the old Hobson's choice of high winds or high bugs. My preference is always high winds. Bring some tent stakes that will work in soft sand, just in case. We oriented our tent with the doors along the wind line and left them open all night with wonderful results. I'm not sure you can do this all the time, but it worked for us in late April.

If you go inland, you'll need reservations for one of the chickees (wooden raised platforms) or ground sites. The chickees are named after the traditional Seminole Indian structures and are 10'x 12' open-sided, roofed buildings with accompanying chemical toilet. If you intend to use these, you'll need a free-standing tent and good bug spray. The ground sites are inland dirt mounds, a few feet higher than the surrounding water, and are usually buggier than the chickees.

Clothing that will give you good sun protection and protect you from the bugs can be very useful (tight weave, lightweight). I like lycra tights for the sun and lightweight pants over them when the bugs get going. Long-sleeved shirts with those fancy openback panels, like the ones they sell for fishing, may also be good. Always bring and use sunscreen wherever you are in Florida, summer or winter.

Bring a good stove. You can cook over an open fire on the beach sites, but you can't really depend on a wood supply in an area that can be wet at any time of the year.

The fishing is probably better than in any other area of the state, but catching them at a time you can eat them is the same problem here as elsewhere. If you intend to stay in one place for a while, think about bringing some form of stringer or net bag to keep fish alive until dinner. A state license for salt and freshwater is required.

4. Weather and Tides

Temperatures will usually be mild in the winter with an occasional cold front down to the low 30s and hot spells into the 80s and 90s (inside). The average low is in the low 60s and the high in the

70s. During the summer, there can be periods of dead calm that will fry your brains until the water whips to a frenzy with a passing thunderstorm. A weather radio is important in this area. Sometimes the reception is bad, but if you try the three available channels (Key West, Miami, and Naples), one should be understandable. Climbing a tall tree helps a lot.

Beware of the tides unless you like slogging through the deepest clay/mud you've ever seen or moving your tent in the middle of the night. Tides can be a major problem, as they can in all the other low-energy coasts around the state. Remember, the MUD is deeper here. Get a tide table and use it (available at Flamingo or Everglades City). Tide lines are easy to spot. Look for the latest line of dead grass and weeds washed up on the beach. Unfortunately, when the winds are blowing, the tide tables seem to go a little haywire. They were off by at least two hours on a few tides last time we paddled. If the tide is running the same way as the wind, expect the lowest tide to arrive later and stay longer. Any tides less than 1' (.9' to -1.5') can be trouble without very careful planning.

5. Friends Along the Way

Don't expect to see a lot of kayakers on the water. Except for some guided tours in the Ten Thousand Islands, the sport just hasn't caught on here yet. It will. Expect to run into a number of local recreational fishermen who motor to many of the beaches along the coast on weekends. I've always found them friendly and willing to share (they can be a good source of cold beer and an occasional fresh fish). Don't go out into these waters expecting help. We saw two boats in two days last time we were out. I like it. You need to remember, you're on your own. Write to Everglades National Park, P.O. Box 279, Homestead, FL 33030, or phone (305) 247-6211, for maps and camping information.

6. My Everglades Trips

Rather than describe the various campsites with some side notes on each as I did for the Big Bend Paddling trail, I thought it would be more helpful to relate the thrilling tales of my actual trips to Everglades National Park. Besides, the campsites are all lovely sandy beaches on the outside that are pretty much the same (camp on one flat sandy place, you've camped on them all. Sort of like if you've seen one redwood, you've seen them all.). Thus, the following will be a real live accounts that you may use to help you or discourage you from taking your next trip to this wondrous area.

TRIP ONE. FEBRUARY 14-18, 1990

I didn't really want to go on this trip. I had just gotten into stained glass and I wanted to stay home and play. My wife said it was time to go, so I did. Six of us planned to paddle together out of Flamingo for a five-day trip. I flew to Miami and stayed with my friend and paddling buddy, Joel, at his house in Coral Gables. We were to meet the other four coming down from Tallahassee at 8:30 the next morning (Wednesday, February 14th) at the boat ramp in Flamingo.

Day 1. February 14, 1990. Joel and I loaded his boat (a fiberglass Easy Rider of early vintage with rear drop skeg) and arrived at Flamingo around 8 a.m., a pleasant two-hour drive down endless interstates from the Gables and 38 miles from the Homestead park entrance. We checked in with the rangers at Flamingo and got the required permit. We went down to the boat ramp and waited. And waited.

They showed up around 10:15 a.m. with a lot of smiles and a story about a brother and a celebration last night in Miami and .... We suggested they get a move on it since the tides were dropping and we weren't exactly sure what we were facing.

I was the titular leader of the group but had only been paddling with the Tallahassee crew once or twice before on flat water. Two were more experienced than the others and had better boats, but none had extensive saltwater or kayak camping experience. (I later found out that two of them had just bought their boats and had never paddled in salt water!) All had camping and canoeing experience so I didn't feel too concerned. Lesson No. 1: Never take inexperienced paddlers to Flamingo and paddle Florida Bay. As the story unfolds, you'll understand why.

We Finally got loaded after a lot of trying. First-time packing for a kayaker can be a slow business. Though they assured us that they had practiced packing before leaving home, it took a little over an hour to load the boats and start paddling out of the harbor.

We encountered our first problem almost immediately. The wind was blowing 15 to 20 knots from the east-northeast and we were going west. As soon as we cleared the harbor entrance the waves started breaking over the sides of the boats and no one had thought to put on their spray skirts (though they were carefully stored nearby). Hey, this is Florida and the temperature was in the 80s and there was no wind in the harbor and the water was shallow. We quickly paddled to shore, sponged out the boats and put on our skirts. This led to the next comic-tragedy. From shore we could see a nice passage between Bradley Key and the mainland with a few motorboats anchored there. If we could make this passage it would save us 20 minutes and allow us to stay closer to shore, out of the wind for a while. Since the novices were already uncomfortable about the high winds and waves, we decided to take a chance. Actually, we asked a couple who were fishing in the motorboat near the passage and they thought we wouldn't have much trouble. Lesson No. 2: Never believe anything anybody in a motorboat tells you. They don't have the slightest idea what a kayak can and can't do and their ideas of mileage rarely seem to have any relationship to reality (this second part is added as an aside from another trip). Well, there was this nice, deep, narrow channel that was going the way we wanted to go, the wind was at our backs, the water was smooth and we sailed. We sailed until the channel ran out, the boats grounded and deep water was only a gleam, about a mile or so away. Our lightest paddler did pole through it and made it to the other side of the bank, where she waved encouragingly. The rest of us were stuck.

Lesson No. 3: Don't step out of your boat on a mud bank in this part of Florida Bay unless you're wearing your scuba tanks. Hey, the boat is bottomed out. How deep can it be? My first step was up to my thigh and the next kept going. I was in deep trouble! I immediately fell over and clutched the top of my boat and floated in the mud for a few minutes, catching my breath. My next move was to swing my legs back into the boat and start wiping off the clay/mud. I then made another stupid decision. I decided to eat lunch (it being 11:30, which is always near enough to lunchtime in my book) and wait out the tides.

After a quick lunch sitting in the boat, I decided to check the tide tables again. Oops, the low was at 2:30, not 12:30. If we waited out the tide, we would be paddling well after dark to reach the campsite we selected or we'd have to turn back and start over the next day. We chose to push on with what I have referred to since as the Everglades "slogg." This is a combination walking, sliding and swimming step you can take while holding onto and pushing the front of your kayak forward anywhere from a few inches to a few feet ahead while the "mudmonster" tries to suck you under, if you make the mistake of trying to rest upright in the mud you continue to sink, so you have to push, kick, and lay across the bow at the same time.

I was wearing my wetsuit booties and had the best protection of all of us, but it was still a miserable experience. Two paddlers went barefoot and cut their feet badly, two others wore tennis shoes and took one step, pulled the shoe out of the mud, took another, pulled the shoe out of the mud, etc. My booties had hook and loop closures so they stayed on for at least three or four steps before they unlatched and filled up with little shell pieces. (When I got back I sewed on longer closures, which solved this problem

We did the Everglades slogg for almost an hour and a half before we hit open water. If we had waited, the area would have become completely dry and we probably wouldn't have gotten off much before 3 or 4 p.m.

We cleaned ourselves and boats as best we could and took off for East Cape Sable, 10 miles away (we actually traveled a little over a mile from the harbor entrance in three hours. If we had left an hour earlier we would have already been at the Cape). With the winds behind us, we started making great time. Lesson No. 4 (no more after this): Certain boats don't paddle very well downwind unless properly loaded. Our two novice novices were paddling Aquaterra Chinooks with straight cut vertical sterns (so was I but I packed better and knew how to handle the waves). The waves were coming from the rear quarter, up to 4′, sometimes breaking over uneven bottoms, bouncing off the shoreline and otherwise just plain nasty. As the waves hit the stern the boats would lift and corkscrew vigorously to one side or the other, I knew they would come back in line with a little rudder and paddling help, but the novices kept overcorrecting, almost turning over when the boat shifted back toward the steering line. They weren't mentally timing the waves so their paddling strokes often came as the boat lifted, giving them purchase on good clean air, which added to their fear and overcorrecting.

Joel was having a different problem. His skeg wasn't big enough to keep his boat tracking straight with the quartering wind. The Easy Rider kept trying to turn left into the wind, and he was forced to paddle almost exclusively on his left side. Not much fun for a two-bladed paddler.

We stopped about halfway to East Cape Sable on the leeward side of the point after East Clubhouse Beach campsite. All of us were exhausted after our slogg except the one who made it through without pushing. Half the crew wanted to turn back. After looking at the waves they would be facing and the time of day (4 p.m., with sunset at 5:30), I convinced them it was better to go on and hope the wind would die down the next day. Right!

The same troubles continued until we made a stupid landfall on the south side of East Cape Sable. The waves were crashing on the beach and the wind was too high for good camping. After exploring around the bend to the north, where good camping was found, four of us re-launched the boats, a hard task as tired as we were. The other two tried to line their boats around the point to the lee. One made it and the other didn't. We did help him empty out the water, however. We camped on East Cape Sable, just down from the old dock. It was a very nice, flat, sandy beach area, above all but hurricane tides, with lots of interesting flotsam and jetsam, and enough driftwood for a nice fire. The wind stayed up, but we had some relief because of the trees that started a hundred feet or so from the beach. There were no bugs. They couldn't fly in this type of wind.

The sun went down with a splashy glow of color soon after we landed so we set up the tents at twilight and fixed supper in the dark (in the light of my trusty Coleman single). During the night I was awakened once by a raccoon sniffing my shoes outside the tent. We had closed off all the food and water in the boats, so there was little to be concerned about. We learned our lesson five years earlier when Joel brought a loaf of bread into his tent while camping on Rock Island in the Big Bend and a coon slit his tent open, ate a few slices of bread, and disappeared into the night.

Day 2. February 15, 1990. The next morning brought more bad news. The winds had actually intensified during the night and the forecast went from a "small craft advisory" to a "small craft caution." They were up to 25 knots with little hope of subsiding. In addition, because of the left side paddling (and lousy pre-trip shape), Joel had spasms on his back during the night and he couldn't straighten up. This is the time that titular trip leaders want to start over or just go home.

We wandered around the beach and helped some fishermen with a swamped motorboat that had been improperly anchored and generally zonked out. We needed to make decisions and nobody wanted to. Joel was in a lot of pain and probably couldn't paddle back. After looking at the alternatives and doing a bit more wandering, we found a fisherman who was willing to take Joel and his boat back to Flamingo. We sent him on his way with all the extra gear (including my dinners, by mistake).

During the early afternoon one of the group went walking along the Cape to the north. He walked about seven or eight miles along the beach and returned exhausted around dinner. He talked about some great walking, but the rest of us weren't very interested by this time.

After Joel was safely on his way I felt great relief. Unfortunately, it didn't solve the other problems facing us. Did we want to paddle on? How would we paddle home with our inexperienced crew? We had another war council. Our options were to paddle further north with the wind and turn around and come back as we had planned, leave now and paddle back to Flamingo, or stay another night and see what the morning brought. We decided on the last alternative.

By late afternoon our moods turned foul again. I tried a little fishing but it was too windy. The weather reports hadn't changed and the winds were just as high as ever. One event did occur that gave us heart. As we walked north of the dock we saw a canoe (can you believe it?) on the beach with a camp full of equipment. We wandered over and found they had paddled that morning from Middle Cape Sable, 5 miles to the north, and the wind in their face was a lot lighter before 10 a.m. in the morning. They were on the water by 5 a.m., and though it was slow going, they were able to make headway.

Now, there is nothing that will make a kayaker puff up faster than to think or insinuate that a canoe could do something his kayak couldn't. We had an immediate war council and decided that we would head back to Flamingo in the morning. Get up at 4:30 and in the boats by 5:00 and off to home.

Dinner was a little happier that night since the decision was made. We shared a lot because my food had gone back with Joel. The wind still howled, leaving that nagging lump in the pit of my stomach, but if the canoers could do it, by golly, so could we.

It was anything but a restful night. Someone was up every hour on the hour testing the wind.

Day 3. February 16, 1990. By 3:30 a.m. the wind had not dropped. None of us had slept because of the hourly reports and the absolutely magnificent sky. It was the sky you see only in the high mountains or on a deserted coast away from city lights. We just decided the canoers were crazy and we might as well get some sleep and try the winds whatever time we got up.

Around 5 a.m., I was awakened by two simultaneous events. The sound of paddles banging against the side of a canoe and the lack of whistling wind. The canoers were right: The wind had dropped significantly (to 15 to 18 knots), so we rolled out of there as fast as we could.

Sunrise was still a few hours away, but we all successfully launched by moonlight and started heading into the wind. There was no problem with the waves. Going into waves is easy. You may not go fast but you can go safely with much less fear of capsizing. Our novices were positively glowing! Five hours later they weren't glowing as much, but we had paddled the 10 miles and took out at the boat basin in Flamingo. We only stopped once or twice on the way back, taking the long way around Bradley Key, but we made it safely, almost anticlimactically. We were, however five tired puppies. The last hour (10 to 11 a.m.) was pure hell. The winds had gone back up to 25 knots with no relief in sight. Our decision to leave early was right. Give canoers a little credit.

TRIP TWO. APRIL 28 TO MAY 1, 1994

My second trip to the Glades was four years later in 1994. I missed my usual winter paddling trip because of a car camping/mountain biking trip to Yellowstone and the canyons of Utah, so I figured I'd have to do something to make up for it The first time I could get off would be the end of April and I knew that was marginal for coastal camping in most of the state. Since it was marginal pretty much everywhere, I decided to try the Everglades again. Maybe this time the weather would cooperate. My paddling buddy Joel had cured his back problems by exercising and had acquired a light, large, comfortable double kayak (Northwest Design, SeaScape II, Kevlar/Graphite, 68 pounds). I only had five days but figured that was probably enough for this time of year. I packed two huge duffels with extraneous but critical gear and flew to Miami. We shopped for food for the trip at the local Publix, did some packing and went to bed early. The tides out of Flamingo looked like about the same as last year, but we weren't taking anyone with us to screw up the schedule so we figured things ought to work out.

We chose Flamingo again because I didn't have enough time to do a long car swap and we wanted an easy trip, somewhere familiar. By this time we had been together on seven or eight camping trips and we were comfortable with each other's styles and needs.

Because we were pretty experienced and relaxed about camping by this time, we decided to take a few new luxuries. A bag of fresh veggies and fruit and no freeze-dried food or Lipton noodle mixes. I even took two mangoes that ripened nicely as we paddled. The crowning glory included a large bottle of wine and five 1.5-liter bottles of Evian each for drinking water. Hey, they were on sale and they fit nicely in the boat! The one thing we left home was my two-burner Coleman butane stove. I just couldn't get it into the duffels for the airplane.

Day 1. April 28, 1994. We got up early and made it to Flamingo by 8:30 a.m. It only took us a half hour to load everything up and get underway. Guess what? The winds were coming from the east-north-east around 15 to 20 knots. This time we had our skirts on before we left the boat basin.

We planned a somewhat different trip because we had more confidence in the boat, no novices along and a little better idea what we might face. Our intention was to paddle southwest (240 degrees) to Carl Ross Key, a designated campsite on an island about 10 miles from Flamingo on the edge of the park next to the Gulf of Mexico. We would spend the night and go north to Middle Cape Sable the next morning, spending two days there exploring, including a day trip to Lake Ingraham. We would then turn south to East Cape Sable for the last night and then home. It sounded nice and relaxed. As usual, it didn't work out that way.

You can't see Carl Ross Key from Flamingo but we were told it would show up as soon as we paddled out a mile or two. The compass heading we followed took us directly toward Murray and Oyster Keys, about 2 miles from Flamingo. Our chart showed some pretty shallow water and we knew we could expect a low tide around 12:30. We vowed we would never push a boat again through the mud of Everglades National Park, so we planned a route that would take us to the north of Oyster Keys, into Sandy Key Basin and through the channel in the First National Bank (lots of jokesters in this area) to Carl Ross.

It actually worked out that way, almost. We stopped off at Murray Key for a pit stop, though the water level was marginal. We paddled next to a 3′ redfish whose fins were half out of the water. As we cleared the Oyster Keys next door, we could see what we thought was Carl Ross Key (and the larger Sandy Key right next to it) in the right direction. Though we harbored doubts, we headed in that direction across the Conchie Channel, always leaving the dark shallow water to our left.

No matter how hard I try, I can never get my mind to work objectively about distances. Things always turn out further away than I expect. I guess I'm an eternal optimist, always thinking the rainbow's a little closer than it is.

This time I forgot about the tail wind. We overshot Sandy Key Basin by a mile or so and in order to cut through the First National Bank we had to go directly into the wind back to the channel entrance. It took us almost 30 minutes of excruciating paddling to go that mile to the two poles that marked the channel entrance. You could see a line of poles marking the channel for a mile almost downwind, but we couldn't get to them without crossing the bank and we were not going to even try.

Once we made the channel entrance, we turned west again and with a 25-knot wind at our backs literally sailed with paddles extended down the channel at around 5 to 7 knots. It was a great rest. Near the end of the channel we turned southwest and ended up on Carl Ross Key around 12:30 p.m.

Carl Ross is a beautiful island. It's crescent shaped, about 1/4 mile long. The main part of the island has a few large mangroves on top of a sand shelf, 8' to 10' above the water. The two ends of the crescent extend as sandy beaches out to the east and the central shelf of the island has some low trees and bushes and many prickly pear cactuses. There's a sign on the south end of the island that tells you its name and allows you to camp. The north end has a picnic table built in under a large mangrove tree.

When we got there, a couple out of Duck Key were getting ready to to leave for home. Bruce and Cathy had a great deal to tell us about the place and helped us with fishing before dinner. They even loaned us their grill to cook our first-night turkey sausage and stingray wing. That's another story for another time, but let me tell you that nobody ever made scallops by plugging stingray wings. I've heard that tale for years and I can finally tell you "it ain't so."

We loved Carl Ross Key. A "drop out" of warblers had just landed from further south and were hopping all over the beach and in the trees and through the open tent. There were 40 or 50 American redstarts along with palm, black-throated blue, black-and-white, and yellow-throated warblers. They danced around you when you ate and sat in the trees just above your head to watch (or ignore) you while you read. I've been birding a long time but I've never experienced anything like this. Out on the flats were a lot of different shorebirds, egrets, and herons, including about 15 reddish egrets of both phases.

We set up our tent under a mangrove tree that was the third in a line toward the east where they blocked off most of the wind. We left the doors open and had no insect problems. The only difficulty we had was with the picnic table. It was on a saddle of the island with nothing to buffer the wind. Anything placed on the table had to be weighted heavily or it was blown into the water. The only time we were able to use the table was for quick projects.

It was a shame because I love to use picnic tables when I camp. I'd load one into the kayak if I could. However, that was the only bad thing about the island. Less wind and that's cured.

I caught some bait in my cast net and went fishing in the afternoon. Bruce and Cathy were catching sharks that were too big for the line they were using, but they seemed to be having fun. It was my usual no-luck day for dinner except for the ray that I don't want to talk about. There were light showers passing over during the night, so we closed the upwind door of the tent. Otherwise it was great sleeping, to the extent first camping nights can be. The temperature started out in the 80s and probably never dropped more than a few degrees the whole time we were on the island.

Day 2. April 29, 1994. We slept a little late because we had no place to go. We decided the island was so nice we'd stay another night. Besides, the wind was still high and we figured it might get a little better if we waited it out. The tide was out most of the morning so we just wandered around, read our books and looked at birds. We intended to visit Sandy Key next door when the tide returned. It would give us a good look at this interesting bird sanctuary, allow us to test ourselves against the wind again, and take up some time in the after noon. Sandy Key is about three to four times the size of Carl Ross and has signs all around it about 100 feet offshore warning you away. The trees on the north end were filled with pelicans, herons, and egrets who appeared in pre-nesting mode. A bald eagle swooped down to the cove on the northeast side as we approached, probably feeding on a dead fish or a hapless egret. It was all we could do to restrain ourselves from landing and beachcombing on a very inviting beach, but we obeyed the rules and made a slow circumnavigation instead. Our temporary island mates assured us yesterday that no one cared if you walked on the island, as long as you didn't camp there. We knew better. There are too few places where people are willing to leave these animals alone. We had our place; they could have theirs. We returned to Carl Ross late in the afternoon and lazed around until dinner. Just before sunset, a 30' sailboat moored about 100 yards off the west side of the island. No one came ashore and we saw no one on board. Sailboats seem to do that. After the sun set, we heard a strange racket in the water that roused us from the tent. A school of 2-to 3-pound skipjacks were passing by in the small channel just off the western point of the island. They would leap, dart forward at high speed, and leap and dart a few more times, one after the other, about 10' from shore. Our flashlights caught their silvery bodies in an eerie glow as hundreds went by. That night we left the tent doors open for a nice breeze and could see glimmers of stars and a late moon through the leaves. No rain. It was a fitting end to a wonderful day.

Day 3. April 30, 1994. We got up early to beat the wind on our way to East Cape Sable. True to form, the winds were in the 15-knot range out of the east. You could easily see East Cape Sable to the northwest of Carl Ross, but we headed due north to the mainland, expecting to be pushed a bit westward as we paddled. The crossing was about 7 to 8 miles with First National Bank on the right to protect us from the worst waves for the first third of the trip.

It was a beautiful morning. Though the winds picked up steadily and pushed small rainstorms over us every few minutes, they were light and the weather was warm enough not to matter. They passed quickly and the sun came out, followed by wonderful rainbows. There was a definite increase in wind prior to each shower (25 to 30 knots), and a definite slowing during the shower before it picked up again to a steady 20-plus knots.

When we passed the bank, the winds and waves picked up. We were securely skirted in but had to paddle dead across the wind, allowing a lot of bouncing and overwash from passing waves. A few sets got as high as 4'. While wallowing through one set, a 25' sailboat motored past in front of us and the captain inquired if we were doing okay with a rather quizzical look. We gave him a thumbs up and kept paddling. (We ran into him a few days later in Flamingo where he was waiting out the wind to continue his journey south. He thought we were crazy.)

We beached at East Cape Sable for a little snack at around 9 a.m. It took us two hours to paddle across. We wandered up and down the beach for a half hour or so and decided to head over to Middle Cape Sable, 4.5 miles away. With a screaming tailwind and high waves (we cut directly across rather than follow the shoreline as safe people would have done), we arrived 45 minutes later, the fastest 4.5 miles of ocean paddling in my life. It was exhilarating, if a little scary.

Middle Cape Sable (I don't know why they don't call them South, Middle, and North, but I don't make the maps) is a large beach on a point of land that sticks out into the Gulf. Behind the beach are colonies of sea oats and cactus for varying distances, some cleared sandy areas and mangrove swamp. We landed on the north side to escape the wind and the eight or nine motorboat campers who had spread out their tents on the beach north and south of Middle Cape. At this point, we made our first big mistake of the trip. We went 100 yards north of the nearest tent to set up camp. We wanted our privacy and besides, we were adventurers and they were boaters - we didn't want to mix.

The mistake was that our tent was too far north of the point to pick up consistent breezes and this day set an April 30 high-temperature record (lower to mid-90s) for Florida's southwest coast. We tried to set up our rain fly for sun protection, but the winds were too strong and erratic. The pegs wouldn't hold in the sand. Where's the parawing when you need it? If we had known how miserable we were going to be, we would have moved the tent in with the other tents near the point (or stayed on Carl Ross). Unfortunately, every time we thought about moving the tent a breeze would come up and we just knew everything was going to be all right. It wasn't. As we got out on the beach, we were greeted by some of the largest horseflies I've ever seen. They were easily 1-1/2" to 2"long. They bit badly, as did their smaller brothers and sisters. The breeze picked up, they would go away. The breeze stopped, they came back. All day long. There was no shade for the tent except back in the mangroves, which we knew was a no-no. We had camp set up by 11 a.m. and had to figure out what to do with the rest of the day. It was too hot and buggy in the tent and too sunny on the beach, so we cast for some bait and tried to fish standing in the water. After paddling 12 miles that morning, standing in the waves with the sun burning down and no fish biting, we were very unhappy campers. We drank a lot of Gatorade, bitched at each other, and tried to figure out what we would do tomorrow. I did catch a mess of jack right off the point on fingerling mullet just before dinner, but decided we weren't hungry enough to eat them. It was the one fun part of the day on Middle Cape. We had no appetite during the day but snacked a little from time to time. Both of us were feeling feverish from the sun and way out of sorts. As the sun started down and the temperatures dropped, our appetites returned and we started being civil to each other again. This was a firm reminder of what summer camping would be like in this area, except that the bugs would be worse.

The motorboaters turned out to be the usual nice people they always seem to be once you settle in and begin to talk to them. They thought we were crazy, of course, but that seems to be usual too. Since we didn't appear threatening, they didn't have trouble with our type of crazy. As the sun went down, one of them even came over and offered us a nice trout for dinner. He was five minutes too late; we had just finished cooking and eating an "interesting" pot-cooked pizza. The weather report for the next day indicated a possible lessening of the winds (15 to 20 knots rather than 20-plus knots) but we weren't convinced. We knew we weren't going to stay another day on this beach. Our options were to go back toward Flamingo and spend the night at some shadier site or go back all the way tomorrow, a day early.

The crowning glory of the day was just after sundown. The horse flies had disappeared, dinner was safely consumed and we were watching the last glow of daylight when every exposed part of my body and some that weren't were covered with mosquitoes. This was not a buildup of bites over a period of time. This was a mass attack, all at once with no warning! Like someone had just opened up a big mosquito box and said "shoo, sic 'em!" I, of course, covered up and sprayed down, and enjoyed that wonderful feeling of about 50 mosquito bites for the next hour or so. A fitting ending to a rotten day.

Day 4. May 1, 1994. We got up at 5 a.m. and left by 6:15, paddling close to shore, south around to East Cape. There must have been some kind of micro-shift in the weather because the wind seemed to be coming from behind us around 5 to 10 knots. The water was flat and lots of fish were feeding in the shallows. We saw a black-necked stilt and other interesting birds along the shore as the sun came up. There were only a few clouds in the sky and no showers in sight. The temperature was in the low 80s.

It took us twice as long to paddle almost the same distance as the day before, even with a slight wind behind us. We got out on East Cape Sable, looking for a shady spot to camp and couldn't find one that would do what we wanted, so we took off around the bend and met the wind in our faces for the next six hours.

The wind started around 15 to 20 knots and built to a steady 20 knots as we paddled. We were making headway, but it was slow going. We stayed as close to shore as we could to deflect some of the wind, but it was too shallow in many places to do that. There were no difficult places, just continuous slow paddling.

A couple of hours later, we reached Clubhouse Beach campsite and stopped for a look around. We might have stayed there but it felt only marginal. I think by this time we had the homelusts and weren't about to stay out with a possibility of bad bugs and sun again. We were just too old for another day of nonsense. We wanted perfect camping to go with perfect paddling or forget it. The area from Clubhouse Beach to East Clubhouse Beach is a beautiful, low plain covered with green succulent plants and small beaches rising above the hard clay/mud, from time to time, in small mangrove coves. There were only a few clumps of mangroves along the shore and a wide-open plain of low plants that seem to flow to the mangrove forest a few hundred yards to a half mile away. It was a visual low garden lawn of light green framed by the blue water on one side and the dark green of mangroves far away on the other. It was truly a unique area. Our problem was whether it would make a good campsite under the conditions. We decided no and moved on.

Three hours later, we stopped in the shallow waters on the northwest point of Bradley Key for a final snack before heading to the boat basin at Flamingo. We were tired but otherwise okay. It was at this point we decided that we would stop this stupid circling of Florida Bay and do a one-way trip with the wind next time or do our circle trip in the Ten Thousand Islands. It was four years since the last trip down, and it will probably be at least four years until the next one. I have lots of other places to see.

TRIP THREE. DECEMBER 10-14, 1997

Day 1. December 10, 1997. I drove down to Everglades City with my wife Casey, our big Northwest Design double, and too much stuff. We were to meet our paddling group at a local motel and start early the next morning. I was a little uneasy about the trip because Casey could no longer paddle for any length of time and I had never tried any distances doing most of the work. I was also in the middle of a major deck remodeling project at our home and really didn't want to leave in the middle of it. On the other hand, this would be my third chance at a better trip in the Everglades and I figured I'd better take it because it's such a neat place and I could prove to myself that my previous experiences were just flukes.

I was convinced to undertake this trip after my two previous unhappy experiences by my brother, Mark (who you may have noticed revised the final chapter in this book). He wanted to try out his new boat and do some kayak camping for the first time. He brought along a friend he was working with (Charlie) who had good paddling and outdoor skills but little kayak camping experience. My old paddling companion, Joel, and his wife, Linda also agreed to come—he because he always goes on my crazy trips and she, to find out why they were always so crazy.

Since this trip was going to be one of the easiest camping trips I've ever tried, having the wives along was probably a good idea. There would be no complaints about leaving them and it would give them some idea of kayak camping in salt water without too much stress. It actually worked out that way.

We all showed up at the motel in time for dinner, an auspicious beginning for our venture. We went to bed early in anticipation of an early wake-up call, and though we only had 7 or 8 miles to paddle, we wanted an early start to have lots of time to play and rest along the way. We weren't sure where we were going to stay for the next four nights but if things worked out, we'd set up base camp at Picnic Key campsite and stay there.

Day 2. December 11, 1997. We got up at 6 a.m. and had a good breakfast at the restaurant next to the motel. From there we drove to the Everglades City ranger station, checked in and put the boats into the water after a very long carry from the parking lot. It was foggy and warm. The temperatures were in the low 80's and mosquitoes were in evidence. The weather report was uncertain though the word "rain" seemed to be mentioned quite prominently from time to time.

Three of us had new GPS units that we could play with at various levels of proficiency. I knew practically nothing about mine other than to enter way points as I went along to help find my way back and check mileage, direction and speed. Mark was better educated in GPS and had a number of the lat/lons of possible campsites already entered; he also understood the other functions. Charlie actually knew how to use his unit and not only had campsite locations entered, but also entered various locations of channels and passages. His expertise was greatly appreciated before the day was finished.

The fog lifted around 10:15 and I took to the water with great anticipation. Well, not really—more like a fond feeling that something not too unpleasant was about to happen. The wind picked up to 10–15 knots from the southwest, helping our crossing of Chokoloskee Bay without too much spray. With skirts in place we didn't ship a lot of water but it did get a bit uncomfortable from the heat build up as we reached the far side a couple of miles or so away. We made it to Indian Key Pass but the water from the incoming tide was coming in so fast that we decided to have a little lunch and wait it out on a nice beach about a 1/4 of a mile up the pass.

When the tide changed, we took off for Picnic Key campsite and had a very leisurely paddle that lasted until around 2:30 p.m., weaving around the many mangrove islands along the way. We would have been lost three or four times without Charley's trusty GPS pointing us in the correct direction because we decided to paddle around the back islands instead of following the pass and turning right when we hit the Gulf. The campsite is a wonderful sandy beach site with a conveniently located portable toilet on skids far enough away not to be a nuisance. Solo paddling the double kayak was easier than I expected.

The many mangrove islands between Everglades City and the Gulf of Mexico are all part of the Ten Thousand Islands, but who's counting. Some have places where you can take out and explore; others are just marshy areas with red and black mangroves that are typical islands of the tropics. Unless you find a nice, sandy beach, don't go there. Even if you can land, the interior of most of the islands are not very hospitable. They also look a lot alike; you can't tell if there's enough water to paddle by using the charts, and you can't gauge the speed of the tides or ease of paddling without venturing forth.

The water around the islands was very active; lots of fish strikes, porpoises in the channels and even a manatee floating lazily by. The main negatives for the whole trip were that it rained each day and the bugs came out at dawn and dusk.

The first night established our pattern for the trip. We ate early and went to bed when the bugs got too bad. I slept well except when the noise from the off and on rain showers beat on the tent during the night. All in all, it was a pleasant but not exciting day.

Day 3, December 12, 1997. The next day we caught some bait (cast net) and went fishing. Though we managed to hook a lot of catfish we weren't enthused about trying to clean and eat them so we gave up fishing and lounged around the beach and read. The temperature was in the low 80s and the sun was hot. The wind started to blow again in the afternoon (10–15 knots) and it kicked up enough surf so that casual paddling was more of an effort than we wanted.

We did explore a little when the early onset of hunger for dinner was a bit too much. We got some more bait and shared it with a couple who had come in at the next key in a canoe. We tried more fishing but gave up soon and let the bait go. The waves had increased and it just wasn't working out. We did cook a great dinner of fresh pizza for everyone. After dinner we spent most of our time trying to keep the raccoons from stealing the rest of our food until we were able to pack it away safely in the hatches. I was afraid we might need bear proof containers but the closed hatches seemed to work. The coons were so tame they walked right through the campsite and almost over my feet. Even strategically thrown shells didn't seem to deter them. If you were lucky enough to hit one, they would just look at you with distain and continue whatever they were doing. We could still hear them rooting around when we went to bed.

Day 4. December 13, 1997. We got up early to warm temperatures (70s) and overcast skies. We tried a little fishing again with no results. When it started to rain, we went back to camp and sat under a tarp shelter for the rest of the day. Storms kept moving through with 15–20 knot winds and high surf. We tried to go out and paddle a while between showers but never quite made it before the next one rolled through. It was not an unpleasant day, sitting around and talking but little to write about. We went to bed early to escape the latest storm.

Day 5. December 14, 1997. It was still raining when we got up early the next morning. The temperatures hadn't dropped much so the rain wasn't too uncomfortable, just annoying. We had planned to stay another night but decided to go home after breakfast, more from boredom than discomfort. We packed up under the rain tarp, leaving our spare water in the portable toilet to reduce weight and help those who came after. The winds had kicked up to 15–20 from the northwest so we had a rough start with 3–4 foot waves, but everything smoothed out when we hit the channel back to Everglades City. I expected the crossing of Chokoloskee Bay to be trouble, but it wasn't. The tail wind and incoming tides carried us across with dispatch.

The most exciting part of the trip was at the boat ramp where Mark tried to walk in to the grassy elevated mound from where his boat bottomed out, about ten feet from the landing. He sank up to mid thigh and got mighty nasty, thrashing his way in. However, his trials helped the rest of us after we tossed him bow lines so that we could be pulled in to disembark on dry land. So much for excitement.

I learned a great deal from this trip. First, I learned I shouldn't go kayak camping unless I was mentally into it. Second, I learned that I no longer enjoy (if I ever did) sitting on a beach for long periods of time watching waves come in while swatting mosquitoes, and I really don't enjoy it if it rains, even with good friends. Third, I don't like camping when the temperature doesn't cool off enough. Fourth, the southern part of the state is not my place.

Summary

I don't know whether I just like paddling in North Florida better or I've been unlucky in Everglades National Park and need to keep trying. There are paddlers who really love this place. Maybe you'll be one of them.

Chapter 15

BIG BEND SEA GRASSES PADDLING TRAIL

This is my coast. I live south of Tallahassee on the St. Marks River, around 15 miles from Apalachee Bay. (See Illustration # 15-1.) Much of my sea kayaking/camping experience comes from this area and I like it a lot.

The whole Big Bend coast covers around 185 miles from the Ochlockonee River in the north to the small town of Bayport in the south. The bottoms are generally covered with sea grasses and the coast line is marsh grass backed with palm/hardwood hammocks and a few mangroves in the south. The beaches are small and occasional, often the product of Native American habitation or coastal creeks or river sand spits. The beaches change with regularity after each big hurricane. The coast is dotted with small villages of fishermen or weekend cottages, usually at the mouths of rivers or back behind the marsh grasses along access creeks that are only navigable at high tide. The water is filled with Styrofoam crab pot markers and strange poles placed in odd places that usually mark some oyster bar, rock or channel.

The motorboats along this coast are mostly recreational boats or small flat-bottom skiffs used by mullet fishermen and crabbers who are common at all hours of the day or night except on weekends. They rarely cause paddlers any trouble and are usually helpful and friendly if you get into trouble. The biggest problem with commercial and recreational fishermen comes from the airboats

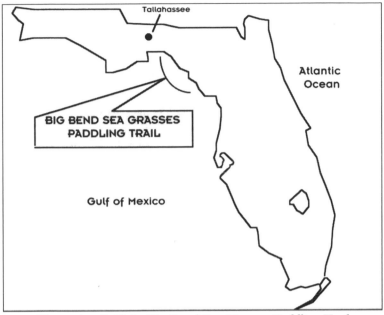

Illustration # 15-1. Big Bend Sea Grasses Paddling Trail

that are noisy and operate in shallower water than you expect. Don't mess with anyone's crab pots and watch out for the airboats.

A trip along the whole Big Bend coast will take a few weeks, depending on how fast you want to do it. Ten to twelve miles a day will give you an opportunity to feel the coast without hurrying and allow you to travel far enough to find campsites to your liking. Every other day will bring you to some village for resupply, refreshment, and an occasional shower.

Be prepared for cold weather The temperature can fall into the upper teens during an extreme event and will be in the 30s at least once during any two-week period from mid-December to March. Freezing temperatures can occur anywhere from late October to mid-April. You can also hit days in the 80s and even an occasional 90 during this period. Most of the time you can expect 60s during the day and 40s during the night as an average.

Though we usually don't get long periods of heavy rains during this time, most passing fronts will produce some rain as they approach (the warm kind) or after they pass (the cold kind). My overall suggestion is to prepare as you would for a trip to south-

Yellowstone in the summer (without the afternoon thunderstorms). Of course, I could be wrong.

Camping on state lands is permitted at designated sites only (see maps for location and GPS coordinates). Camping on Federal land (St. Marks and Lower Suwannee National Wildlife Refuges) is not permitted at all because they are wildlife refuges. However, emergency camping spots are easy to locate from the boat when you're close. Just look for tall trees near the water (or small gray areas next to the water on your nautical charts). Since most of this coast is marsh grass, the trees are relatively easy to spot. Don't expect to pull through the marsh grass to reach a camping spot in those trees you see in the distance. It's very rare that trees on the back side of the marsh contain a lot of high ground right away. There may be an additional quarter of a mile of trees before it's high enough to camp on. However, if the trees come down to the water, there are usually beaches or Indian middens that stay above water at all but the highest tides.

There are some camping spots in the St. Marks National Wildlife Refuge and we may see some in the Suwannee as well in a few years. If you have a special need to camp on some of the federal land, write and ask permission first.

St. Marks NWR - P.O. Box 68, St. Marks, FL 32355
Lower Suwannee NWR - Rt. 1, Box 1193c, Chiefland, FL 32626

Chassahowitzka NWR (Crystal River NWR)
1502 S.E. Kings Bay Dr., Crystal River, FL 34429

Some camping spots are located on county-owned lands (Shired Island, Horseshoe Beach, and Keaton Beach) while others are on private land, not available to the public above the mean high tide line. As long as you're away from the inhabited areas and keep your campsite clean, no one seems to mind if you spend the night while passing through. However, if you plan to stay for a while, find a good legal place.

There are some very good seafood restaurants in the small villages. Though the quality goes up and down with new owners, it all tastes great after a few days in a boat. The only question you have to answer is whether it's worth paddling up the rivers to reach them. Keaton Beach, Steinhatchee, Horseshoe Beach, Suwannee, and Cedar Key are the most accessible. Restaurants there change ownerships rapidly and it's hard to keep up with who is and isn't in business. However, someone is usually open during most of the year in each place.

One more short note about the tides (this is a repeat): The Big Bend coast is a very shallow, low-sloping shoreline in most places. Though the tides are not extreme by Bay of Fundy standards, they can cause you a LOT of trouble. Plan every day with the tide tables in front of you or make sure you have lots of time. Three- or four- hour delays are not unusual, even for kayaks, unless you like a lot of mud pulling. Plan some night paddles, if necessary. Be flexible and you'll do just fine.

The following narrative includes a brief description of the designated and non-designated campsites along the Big Bend Historic Saltwater Paddling Trail that was designated by the Florida Legislature in 1992 and extended south to the Withlacoochee River in Yankeetown in 2003. It's approximately 105 miles long from the mouth of the St. Marks River to the mouth of the Withlacoochee River in Yankeetown, Levy County. However, paddling to and from all campsites, the total paddling distance is approximately 160 miles. A mileage chart (see illustration # 15-2) shows the distances between designated campsites with GPS coordinates. Non-designated campsites are discussed on the following pages but are not included in the mileage chart. I have either camped or personally walked on many of the campsites; however, because of storms, be prepared to choose an alternative in case one has been washed out. Do exploratory day trips in questionable areas to help familiarize yourself with the present river entrance markers and conditions. Also, side trips on tidal creeks are extremely scenic and worthwhile ventures. Plan a few extra days to enjoy these opportunities. The site numbers are for convenience only. If you try to do them in order, you're in for a very long and difficult trip. Use the accompanying maps to help you with trip planning, but buy the appropriate U.S. Government NOAA nautical charts for navigation at your local marina or tackle store. Look for the guide book on the Big Bend Historic

Saltwater Paddling Trail, prepared by the Florida Fish & Wildlife Conservation Commission (FFWCC). It contains maps, campsite locations and lots of information and photographs about the trail. A good road map is a must. The maps in this book and the navigation charts help but don't precisely identify access points from your location around the state. A road map may also help you with emergency decisions. The last time I looked, it took three of those expensive charts to do the whole Big Bend trail. New maps referenced above are a worthwhile purchase. (See Chart # 11405–Apalachee Bay, # 1407–Horseshoe Point to Rock Island, and # 11408–Crystal River to Horseshoe Point.)

The site numbers may appear strange to you, starting with "0" and including some pluses and minuses. These are the numbers we turned in for use by the state in setting up the paddling trail. I confess to being responsible for these numbers and now it's just easier not to change them to a more logical format.

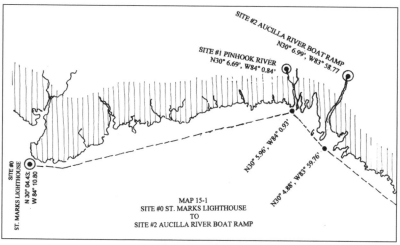

Map # 15-1.

1. St. Marks Lighthouse to Aucilla River

Site #0. St. Marks Lighthouse. There are no campsites near the river entrance of the St. Marks River. The closest one is 11 miles run by the Florida Department of Agriculture with restrooms

Big Bend Saltwater Paddling Trail Site Mileage Chart

Site Number and Name	GPS Coordinates	Next Site	Nautical Miles To Next Site
0. St. Marks Lighthouse	N 30° 04.432' W 84° 10.807'	Pinhook River	11
1. Pinhook River	N 30° 05.931' W 84° 0.962'	Aucilla Boat Ramp	6.7
2. Aucilla River Boat Ramp	N 30° 06.99' W 83° 58.77'	Econfina Campground	10
3. Econfina Campground	N 30° 03.52' W 83° 54.40'	Rock Island Campsite	9.7
4. Rock Island Campsite	N 29° 58.33' W 83° 49.79'	Spring Warrior Campsite	11
5. Spring Warrior Campsite	N 29° 55.13' W 83° 39.85'	Keaton Beach	10
6. Keaton Beach	N 29° 49.17' W 83° 35.60'	Sponge Point Campsite	3.5
7. Sponge Point Campsite	N 29° 46.76' W 83° 35.22'	Dallus Creek Campsite	7.8
8. Dallus Creek Campsite	N 29° 42.83' W 83° 29.90'	Steinhatchee	7.8
9. Steinhatchee	N 29° 40.401' W 83° 23.770'	Sink Creek Campsite	9.8
10. Sink Creek Campsite	N 29° 33.40' W 83° 24.10'	Horseshoe Beach Campground	12
11. Horseshoe Beach Campground	N 29° 26.40' W 83° 17.60'	Butler Island Campsite	2
12. Butler Island Campsite	N 29° 25.87' W 83° 16.18'	Shired Island Campground	5
13. Shired Island Campground	N 29° 23.60' W 83° 12.12'	Salt Creek Ramp	5
14. Salt Creek Ramp	N 29° 19.71' W 83° 09.99'	Clark Island Campsite	6.7
15. Clark Island Campsite	N 29° 14.373' W 83° 03.82'	Shell Mound	10.8
16. Shell Mound	N 29° 19.452' W 83° 04.152'	Cedar Key Ramp @ #4 Channel Bridge	3
17. #4 Channel Bridge	N 29° 09.88' W 83° 01.63'	Kelly Creek Campsite	5
18. Kelly Creek Campsite	N 29° 0.975' W 82° 53.06'	Turtle Creek Campsite	10
19. Turtle Creek Campsite	N 29° 06.708' W 82° 46.333'	Yankeetown Boat Ramp	9
20. Yankeetown Boat Ramp	N 29° 0.116' W 82° 45.724'		11.7

and tables but a little far to start from unless you want a very long first day. It's also a little noisy from the highway traffic. However, if you get there when the bikers come through on their way to speed week in Daytona Beach, it's very exciting. There's also the best smoked mullet in the world at Outz's bar just across the river. If you intend to do the whole trail, you'll probably want to start at the St. Marks Lighthouse, which is about 9 miles from U.S. 98 on a clearly marked paved road (S.R. 59) that passes the St. Marks Wildlife Refuge visitors center. Look at the birds and ducks in the ponds on the way and get a quick preview of some of the wildlife you'll see on the trail. The turnoff is to the south, just east of the St. Marks River Bridge on U.S. 98.

If you turn right on the paved road a few hundred yards before you get to the lighthouse, you can launch at a concrete slab boat ramp that's very rough on boats and feet. If this doesn't appeal to you, drive all the way to the end of the road and launch at the small beach to the right of the lighthouse parking lot. When the tide is out, the boat ramp is preferable unless you like carrying a long way.

Site #1. Pinhook River (Map 15-1). 11 nautical (n.) miles from the St. Marks Lighthouse. This is a beautiful primitive camp-site area that's for special use by the hikers along the Florida National Scenic Trail that passes along this part of the coast. It's not easy to get to and may be out of your way, but could be a good practice overnight for a later trip.

For the first few miles, you paddle along pleasant narrow beaches and hammocks that shield substantial marsh grasses and salt flats behind. These beaches are cut in a few places by small salt creeks. Don't get used to this scenery. It changes to salt marsh a few miles down the coast, never to return. No camping is allowed in this part of the refuge. Keep careful track of your map and turn north into the Pinhook river, about 8 to 9 miles down the coast. Paddle up the Pinhook (stay to the left fork) about 2 miles until you come to a small bridge. The river is narrow with sharp lime-stone outcroppings at low tide. Some log portaging may be required as well.

The takeout point will depend on the tide level. If the water is high, you may try paddling under the bridge and turning to the left as far as you can along a canal. You might actually make the campsite under extreme conditions. However, you probably won't be able to leave until the next high tide unless you want a very long and painful drag. The most dependable take-out seems to be from the bridge fill area on the right on the upstream part. Look around and find what's best for you.

The campsite is located about 100 yards from the bridge. Carry your gear down the maintained grassy road to the left (west) and cross a log bridge across the canal on the right (north). The campsites are under the trees on a pine needle cushioned area just after the log bridge. There should be room for ten or fifteen tents. If you intend to use this site, you should notify the Refuge people at the visitors center when you pass by to launch.

Site #2. Aucilla River Boat Ramp (Map 15-1). 12 n. miles from the St. Marks Lighthouse. There are a number of sites along the Aucilla but none should be used except in emergencies. They are all a few miles upriver and are either in the St. Marks Wildlife Refuge or on private land. None are available for camping without permission. We hope to see some of these open to the paddler in the future. There's little to remark on about paddling along this section of the coast. Lots of marsh grasses, mud flats, oyster bars, and open water. There are a few large rocks (a few square feet across) a mile or two offshore that are visited by birds and redfish, but few kayakers. It's usually peaceful and filled with birds, ducks, and crab traps during the winter.

The mouth of the Aucilla River is marked by some type of pole structure or light system, depending on when the last storm was and the amount of damage done. There's a fair amount of traffic on the river, so finding the entrance should not be difficult. If you come over from the Pinhook, you can take the cutoff shown on the maps. About a mile from the mouth, the river narrows and the banks change from salt marsh to palm and hardwood hammocks. You can camp on any dry spot in an emergency, but otherwise consider this a marginal area. The river water is salty a long way from the Gulf, depending on the height of the tides. Don't depend on it for fresh water. Some of the houses may be willing to let you have some well water (if anyone is home) but even this water isn't all that great.

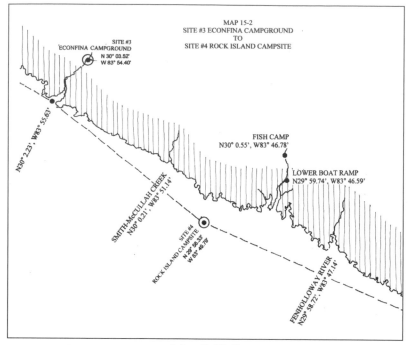

Map # 15-2.

2. Econfina River to the Fenholloway River

Site #3. Econfina Campground (Map 15-2). The official campsite on the Econfina is part of a new, proposed state park. It's now run as a private campground next to Econfina-on-the-Gulf, a small store, motel, and housing development. The state park should be finished in a few years. The campground has lots of room. The campground is located under the oaks, about 2 miles from the river entrance. The Econfina River looks much like the Aucilla with its marsh grasses near the Gulf and palm and hardwood hammocks as you go inland. The river entrance is marked with some form of pole, or poles, but I won't describe them because they change all the time. There is no official channel. Usually, some bright fisherman will hang a colorful plastic detergent bottle on the pole to make it more visible.

Econfina River Bank Sites. There are a number of one-tent sites starting about a mile up from the river entrance that are on state-owned lands. You can use them for camping as long as the park hasn't officially opened. These are next to the river on small parcels under the red cedar trees. Check them out on the way upriver. I've seen people using these, but I doubt you can depend on them because of the changing conditions of the river. They are also noisy and exposed to river traffic, which can be high at certain times of the year. Some of these sites are quite illusory. They look dry but are mainly composed of leaf drop and grass wash-ins at high tide. You can fall through right to water if you're not careful.

Side Trip to Hickory Mound. 7.5n. miles from the Econfina campground. This site is located a mile up what is referred to on some maps as Smith-McCullah Creek. The site is not officially permitted for camping because it's on a dike impoundment that's part of a Wildlife Management Area. The best camping would be next to the dirt road on the top of the dike, near the boat ramp.

The entrance to Smith-McCullah Creek is hard to find, but like most access points along this coast, there's usually a post of some sort at the entrance. You can also see a utility pole with a transformer on it near the boat ramp to help guarantee you're at the right place. The GPS coordinates of the creek entrance are N30° 0.21,′ W83° 51.14′ (Map 15-2). The creek is very shallow at low tide so expect to drag a little if you miss the tide. The impoundment dike area is used for crabbing and fishing in the summer and is a great birdwatching spot. It's not patrolled very heavily, so if you need to camp there in an emergency, it shouldn't be a problem. If you know you intend to camp there as part of your trip, call the Florida Fish and Wildlife Conservation Commission (FFWCC) office in Tallahassee for permission.

Little Rock Island. 3.5 n. miles from Hickory Mound and 10 to 11 from the Econfina campground. This is a small (5- acre) island, about a mile off the coast, a few hundred yards from Rock Island to the south. It has some upland vegetation but is mostly marsh and relatively undisturbed. This island could be used in an extreme emergency for one or two tents, but should be avoided if possible.

Site #4. Rock Island (Map 15-2). 3.5 n. miles from hickory Mound and 10 to 11 from the Econfina campground. This site is one of the wonders of the whole Big Bend paddling experience. It's a 20-plus acre island, a little more than a mile from shore, that has more amenities, little areas of interest and just plain good feelings than any other site in the area. This description could be purely personal because I stayed there the first night camping on my first kayak camping trip after an unexpectedly long paddling day. I did go back later, however, and felt the same way about it.

The approach to the island should be from the west, where you'll see two sloping cuts in the limerock that are what substitute for a beach in this low-energy area. At low tide you have 15' to 20' of beach that's reduced to 4' to 5' at high tide. The island is 2' to 3'above water even at the highest tides (hurricanes excepted). The locals claim the Indians made these cuts so they could land easier on the island. I'm very suspicious of that since they seem natural and these islands might have been connected to the mainland in the not-too-distant past. I've found pot shards and flint chips on the island, so I know it was inhabited by Native Americans, but unless the Indians had some type of dynamite and then smoothed the edges down on the limestone, I doubt the stories are true.

The best camping on the island is the flat grassy area above the cuts on the west side. There is room for ten or more tents without crowding. There is a small freshwater marsh (1 acre) behind the grove of dwarfed oak trees that line the east of the grassy area and a salt marsh covering most of the east side of the island. You can expect a lot of mosquitoes during warm weather. On the south side there are a series of remarkable tidal pools formed out of the limerock and filled by high tides and rainwater. They seem to contain some unique ecosystems I've not seen anywhere else in the area—lots of different aquatic plants and animals.

The island is used frequently by fishers and their families and has been badly trashed from time to time, but it is usually cleaned up when things begin to overflow. A hurricane in 1985 rolled about a billion beer cans and pop bottles onto the island, but they seemed to have been cleaned up a few years later.

If this island were not located so close to the Fenholloway River (the oozing pustule of the Big Bend), it would be a perfect place to settle for a few days and relax and fish. Unfortunately, the water around the island can be dark from the river and the fish caught in the area are suspect. Ah, there is no paradise in paradise!

Fenholloway Boat Ramp is not a designated campsite, but available for emergencies, and if time permits a short side trip 5 n. miles from Rock Island, about 2 miles from the river entrance (Map 15-2). It is a primitive commercial campsite and fish camp with chemical toilets and a few picnic tables. The site is in a large hardwood hammock on the banks of the river. The Fenholloway River is Florida's only classified industrial river. During periods of low rainfall, most of its flow comes from the paper mill upstream. It's dark, dirty, and often very smelly. The fish and alligators look funny and unless you're in real trouble, or a toxic waste junkie, you should avoid this river.

Lower Fenholloway Boat Ramp. 4 n. miles from Rock Island, a mile upriver from the entrance (Map 15-2). This land is owned by a large paper company which generally doesn't care if you camp on its property as long as you don't trash it. There are a few tent sites next to the boat ramp on filled land. For the reasons expressed above it isn't a very nice river, though the land area is quite pretty. There's some local traffic here on weekends, and Saturday nights could be loud and raucous. You may be more interested in this site as a takeoff or pickup point than a campsite. The only reason I know about either site is that I drove here one day. I've never paddled the river, not being a toxic waste junkie. Others have and told me it's quite scenic with lots of alligators near the river mouth.

3. Spring Warrior to Sponge Point (See Map # 15-3.)

Site #5. Spring Warrior Campsite (Map 15-3). 11 n. miles from Rock Island and Fenholloway sites. This is one of those strange clusters of dwellings, common along this coast, about 1.5 miles upriver along Spring Warrior Creek. The entrance will be marked by some kind of pole or poles since there is a fair amount of traffic in and out of the creek. The last time I was there, the creek mouth was marked with a 10'-high tripod of telephone poles with a large detergent bottle tied to the top. You can probably see some of the houses set back in the marsh as you paddle up to the shoreline. You may have to drag your boat through the creek mouth at some low tides, but the rest of the creek is fairly deep.

Upriver there's a concrete boat ramp, a number of weekend cottages and possibly a small store and some rental cottages as well. Continue past the boat ramp to the designated campsite. Don't depend on Spring Warrior for any amenities and you'll probably be pleasantly surprised. Plan on them and you could be in bad trouble. The people are usually friendly and camping shouldn't be a problem if you're polite about it. All of the area that's high and dry is private, so ask permission first. With a name like "Spring Warrior Camp" it's hard to pass up this one.

Yates Creek (Map 15-3). 3.5 n. miles from Spring Warrior Camp. This is a marginal campsite next to a boat ramp on a small tidal creek. There is a small beach next to the water for hauling out. Access is difficult at low tide.

Adams Beach (Map 15-3). 2.5 n. miles from Yates Creek. This is another marginal campsite because it's possibly on private land next to the end of a county road. It's not a bad launch or take-out point except at low tide. You could camp near the road on county property if no one from the county is there to run you off. This site is the beginning of the area where private homes and small communities prevail. The site itself has little construction around it, but from here on down the coast for the next 12 to 14 miles, houses abound. If you come in at dusk, clean up well, and leave early, it's doubtful anyone would know you were there.

Adams Beach Annex (Map 15-3). 1.1 miles from Adams Beach up a small tidal creek. There's room for three to four tents on a flat area near the boat ramp about 200 yards from the Gulf. Land access is from a dirt road off the hard road that leads to Adams Beach. The dirt road runs through someone's front yard, so take it slow. The owner chased us down last time because we were so inconsiderate of his animals. We didn't know it was a front yard

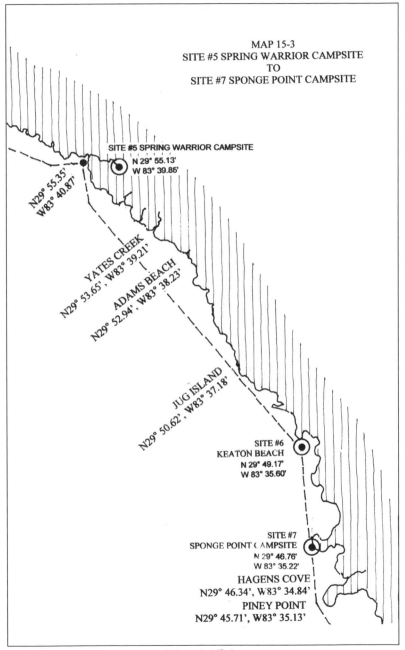

MAP 15-3
SITE #5 SPRING WARRIOR CAMPSITE
TO
SITE #7 SPONGE POINT CAMPSITE

SITE #5 SPRING WARRIOR CAMPSITE
N 29° 55.13'
W 83° 39.85'

N29° 55.35'
W83° 40.87'

YATES CREEK
N29° 53.65', W83° 39.21'

ADAMS BEACH
N29° 52.94', W83° 38.23'

JUG ISLAND
N29° 50.62', W83° 37.18'

SITE #6
KEATON BEACH
N 29° 49.17'
W 83° 35.60'

SITE #7
SPONGE POINT CAMPSITE
N 29° 46.76'
W 83° 35.22'

HAGENS COVE
N29° 46.34', W83° 34.84'

PINEY POINT
N29° 45.71', W83° 35.13'

Map # 15-3.

at the time (you had to be there). The campsite is probably on county property, but check around and see if anyone objects before you use this site.

Jug Island. 2.5 miles from Adams Beach Annex (Map 15-3). This is really just a beach on a point of land that's privately owned and surrounded by houses. Named islands on this part of the coast often mean higher land that is connected to the mainland by marsh grasses which may be partially covered at higher tides. They look like islands when you're far out to sea and the marsh grasses are below your sight horizon. I mention this site only because it's high ground and near the coast. It could be used as an emergency campsite or lunch stop.

Site #6. Keaton Beach (Map 15-3). 2 miles from Jug Island around the corner to the east. This is the public beach for the village of Keaton Beach. The beach is owned and maintained by Taylor County and has picnic tables, restrooms, and running water. The beach was dredged up years ago when the channel next to it was dug, but it's a very pleasant place to stop or camp. We called the Taylor County administrator to get permission to camp on the beach for a night and he didn't seem very concerned. I can't advise paddlers to camp at this spot without first checking with the county, but like many places along this coast, if you come in quietly, camp quickly, and clean and leave in the morning, no one will bother you.

The approach to Keaton Beach is hard to miss. Though there was a wild winter storm that destroyed a number of buildings and houses in 1993, this village is pretty obvious from the water. Just follow the shoreline around to the east and you'll come to the south-facing beach. The town has a few stores, restaurants with wonderful seafood, and some motel rooms. You can also get water at the park, use a telephone down the street, and walk a paved road if your senses have been too deprived of urban living for a while. On our 1985 trip, the reporter from the Tallahassee newspaper who paddled with us watched three bald eagles circle her as she phoned in her story from this phone. The place has very good karma.

I would like to give you a directory of available services here, but everything is too transitory to do that. The village is a single

paved street about a half mile long that connects to the local county roads. The beach is a good launching place at high tide and a bit
muddy at low. Even if you don't camp here, it's a great place to stop
for lunch, either from your lunch bag at the picnic table, or at a
local restaurant. You can also get the latest fishing reports and gear
as well as boat repairs at the local marinas. I've always found this a
friendly place to stop and spend some time.

The paddle from Spring Warrior to Keaton Beach shows some
general changes in direction and bottom conditions. You go from
mainly east/west to south/north as you turn the corner of the Big
Bend. This usually gives you better alignment with the prevailing
winds in the winter or shelters you from the direct easterlies. The
bottom slope is shallower with lots of little rock heads sticking up
in the north part. The water clarity improves a little. The submerged grasses are abundant, but they seem a little thinner in many
places and disappear entirely as you approach a developed area.

The bird life away from shore in this area can be awesome. A
day of paddling in the winter can be broken up by sightings of
ducks you may not see many other places. We approached Keaton
Beach one time and started diverting around what looked like a
half-mile-long oyster bar that didn't appear on any map. As we got
closer we discovered the whole "bar" was in motion. It was 2,000
to 3,000 Redhead ducks that had just landed from the north and
were busily feeding on bottom vegetation. As we approached, they
took off with an amazing wing sound that few are privileged to
hear. Next time, we'll give them a wider berth and hope we don't
disturb their feeding. More mundane sightings of small flocks of
buffleheads, red-breasted mergansers, hooded mergansers, double-
crested cormorants and loons occurred all day as they continuously dove or flew out of the way as we approached.

This is also a good area to see bottlenose dolphins (as are most
areas of the Big Bend). They'll often appear when you least expect
them and stay with you for a while, as long as you don't approach
too close. They probably won't be in water shallower than 3' unless
they're chasing fish at high tide.

Site #7. Sponge Point (Map 15-3) is now a designated campsite along the Trail. It's 3.5 n. miles from Keaton Beach on a point

of land with a small beach, nice grassy area, and small oak/palm hammock. It's connected to the mainland by a marsh area that can be traversed by four-wheel-drive vehicles at low tide. Since the area has been purchased by the state and is managed by Florida Fish and Wildlife Conservation Commission (FFWCC), most of this traffic has been stopped.

It's a very nice campsite with room for four to five tents on the grassy area between the beach and the hammock. This is one of the better campsites away from human interference. It's sometimes used by fishers but usually it's just a picnic spot for folks who launch at Hagens Cove. This site is part of a complex that includes Sponge Point, Hagens Cove, Piney Point, and Piney Point Annex. All of these sites are within 3 miles of each other and are part of lands managed by the FFWCC. This one is the best campsite of the four.

The bottom slope approach to Sponge Point is better than Hagens Cove and about the same as Piney Point across the way. It's great at high tide and bearable at a normal low. We woke once on a foggy morning and couldn't see water in any direction. We waited a few hours and it came in as the fog lifted. Don't be in a hurry unless you plan your tides well (don't hurry then, either).

Hagens Cove (Map 15-3). 9 n. miles from Sponge point. This is a maintained recreation area with covered picnic tables, chemical toilets, a boat ramp, and grassy play area. The ramp is about 2 miles down a dirt road from SR 361. No camping is permitted, but emergencies will be overlooked. Access after dark is restricted. There are no commercial facilities here.

The cove is very shallow with most of the bottom exposed at lower low tides. It's a great birding area. I counted over 30 great blue herons wading around the cove one morning before leaving Sponge Point for places south. In the summer, this is a good location to put in for scalloping if areas closer to home are not producing. The cove cuts in far enough to the east that paddlers heading south from Keaton Beach will often miss it. Looking from kayak height, if you pass a few hundred yards off Sponge Point, all you can see are some ill-defined structures unless you use binoculars. Don't stop here for a visit unless you have the tides with you. A mistake here and you may have a long wait or a long, long muddy drag.

Piney Point. 1.2 n. miles from Sponge Point, .9 miles from Hagens Cove. This is a larger high-ground area than Sponge Point, but has little open low grassy areas for camping. The grasses are waist high with a lot of low brushy bushes around a nice pine grove. There has been little or no camping on this point in a long time, so anyone who wants to camp here will have to make his/her own smooth area. Since Sponge Point is now available, I wouldn't use this site because of a built-in aversion to messing with the native vegetation when I don't have to. In order to minimize disturbances, camp near the small beach line. The tides here are the same as at Sponge Point.

Piney Point Annex. 0.5 miles around the bend from Piney Point. This site is a narrow hammock band with a small beach that runs a few hundred yards along the shore. It contains the usual oaks and cedars with a lot of prickly pear cactus understory. Some nice campsites are available near the beach under the trees. Watch out for the cactus and low tides.

4. Dallus Creek to Steinhatchee (See Map # 15-4.)

Site #8. Dallus Creek Campsite (Map 15-4) is a FFWCC designated site on the north entrance to Dallus Creek. It's the usual hammock and small beach site but because it's rarely used, is a bit overgrown. Behind this site is a grassy area that could be okay for a few more tents. The bugs were bad the day we camped here because the temperature was in the 70s during the day and only dropped 10 degrees at night. This was late December, so beware. This site could get wet with an unusually high tide and westerly wind. It's a few hundred yards from the Dallus Creek channel with lots of mud between. At lower low tides, you would have to pull over the whole distance to the channel, paddle a short way and then pull over the blockage at the entrance. Wait out the tides. We had to wait four hours after dead low to get out of here.

Dallus Creek Upriver (Map 15-4). 2 miles upriver from Dallus Creek North where the creek reaches the tree line. There

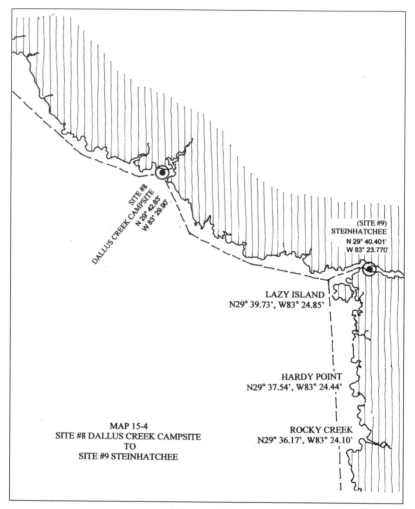

Map # 15-4

is a boat ramp and wonderful live oak grove here with a few picnic tables. There is no official camping permitted here since the FFWCC took over management of Dallus Creek as a wildlife management area. The boat ramp is about 2 miles from SR 361, where a controlled access point for hunters is maintained during the day. In the winter hunting season this is a very heavily used area. The gates at the highway are closed at dark and the area is sometime patrolled for poachers.

Site #9+. Steinhatchee (Map 15-4). 7 n. miles from Dallus Creek North. The largest little village along the paddling trail. It's located mainly on the north side of a fairly wide, if short, coastal river (the Steinhatchee River), about a half mile up from the entrance. It provides all the amenities you would expect, from restaurants, motels, small stores, boat ramps, trailer parks, and commercial camping (at RV places and most motels) to a post office. The place can get crowded on summer weekends and when different fishing seasons open. It's mainly a port for commercial and recreational fishing with a smattering of vacation homes.

Steinhatchee Spoil Island North. Half mile from the Village of Steinhatchee on the north side of the river channel. This spoil island is a surprisingly nice place to camp with room for six to eight tents. It's covered with strange emergent vegetation with lots of thorns in some places and cedar trees and cabbage palms in others. For those of you who don't know, a spoil island is an island formed by dredging spoil material (sand, rock, mud, etc.) from the water bottom and piling it all in one place, usually along a channel. There are a number of these along the Steinhatchee channel to the south, but this is the only one on the north side with trees and high ground for camping. The others are mostly small, rocky islets that go underwater at high tide.

This site is about 10 to 15 acres in size with a small beach on the south side and lots of flat places for camping. Our favorite spot sometimes leaks sap onto your tent. The other advantage to this site is its closeness to the old river channel, allowing you easy access even at low tide. We chose it specifically for that purpose, knowing we were going to have to leave the next morning at a reasonable time in order to get to our next stop. We only had to drag 10 to 20 yards to float the boats and then were forced to paddle a mile and a half out the river channel in order to get enough water to go south. If we had camped at either of the next two sites, we would have had to wait until noon to get out. The disadvantage to this site is the amount of float-in trash and the boat noise during the night. For some reason, the local airboats were using the island as a marking target, speeding toward it at full speed and cutting away at the last minute. After bounding out of the tent to make sure I wasn't going to get run over in the middle of the night the first time this happened, I did okay the next five or six times until it stopped around 2 A.M. I've only camped here once, so I don't know if this represents every night or was a product of some fish happening. My guess is that the fish were running and so were the boats. Restrictions on netting in inshore waters may help with this in the future.

There must be some magic emanating from the island, since while setting up our tents we got a visit from a kayaker from D.C. who just happened to come by for a look at the coast. This was the first kayaker not attached to one of our trips I'd seen along this coast in the nine years I'd been paddling. I'm not a big fan of spoil islands but this one was fun.

Steinhatchee Spoil Island South. 0.5 miles from Steinhatchee Spoil Island North. This island is a high lump of ground to the south of the main channel and may be suitable for one or two tents in an emergency. It's about 20' to 25' high and maybe an acre in size. Don't even think about this one unless you're lost in a storm and very desperate.

Lazy Island (Map 15-4). 0.3 miles south of Steinhatchee Spoil Island South. This is a wonderful place to camp in the Steinhatchee area if you don't have to worry about tides. Six to ten sites for tents. A good-sized white sand beach with a cozy hammock nearby and super ambiance. We ended our 1985 trip on this island and the relief of the finish must have left my psyche with a warm glow that appears every time I think of this place. One of my photos of Lazy Island was published in the Destinations section of Canoe Magazine a few years later, and since they actually paid me for it, you know the memories have to be good.

Lazy Island is also a good place from which to commute to Steinhatchee for resupply and a hot meal. It's only a mile or so and as long as the tides allow, can be used as a base for wilderness camping while enjoying some of the luxuries of civilization. The paddle back at night, with twinkling stars so bright they cast shadows, is a wonderful experience. There are no houses nearby and only the occasional mullet boat to destroy the serenity. I must warn you, however, that if the tides are right and the mullet are running, fishermen have been known to be out all night netting fish by pounding hammers on the side of the boat to scare fish into the nets. It's very disconcerting to be awakened by the sound of hammers on the water a few hundred feet from your tent. This practice has ended now that Florida has adopted restrictions on inshore netting.

Hardy Point (Map 15-4). 2 n. miles from Lazy Island, but only marginal for camping. We couldn't get to shore to walk this site because of low tide, but it shows up on the map as a hammock site on the north side of a cove. Since all the others we saw marked this way turned out to be reasonable, this one could be also. However, if we couldn't get near enough to scout it effectively at low tide, you can bet it's one of those you need to be real careful with.

Rocky Creek (Map 15-4). 5n. miles south of Lazy Island, up a small tidal creek to a boat ramp. The camping is around the ramp. This would be a very buggy site if the weather warmed. It's too far up the creek to get shore breezes and low tides would hamper ingress and egress. I've not been to this site personally, but the paddlers who have seem to think it would be okay. I don't want to recommend any off-the-coast sites unless you need shelter from a storm or it's cold enough to keep the bugs down. Watch out for the rocks at low tide.

Bowlegs Point (Map 15-4). 10 miles from Lazy Island. This is a very good camp spot and should be used instead of the others in the area unless you feel you don't have much choice. There should be room for five to six tents. This is another "island" connected to the mainland by marsh grasses with a large hammock of palms, pines, cedars, and hardwoods. The best camping is found by taking a well-worn path on the north side of the hammock, behind the tidal pool, into the trees. Once inside you should see open areas for tents plus some rough table and chair constructs built by bored fishers. There's a fair amount of trash, but ignore it if you can. Some people can't help themselves (right!).

The beach is a little soft, but it didn't seem to be an inordinate mud pull to get out, even at low tide. There's good exploring around the area and reputed good fishing.

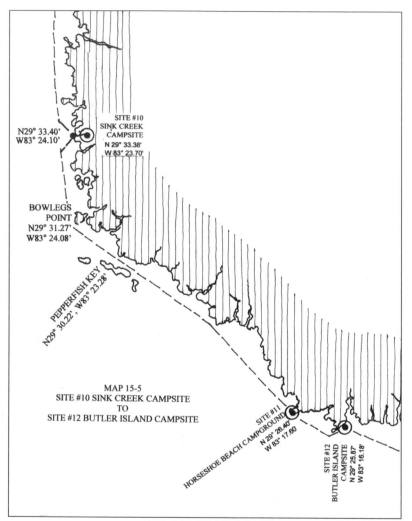

Map # 15-5

5. Sink Creek to Butler Island

Site #10. Sink Creek (Map 15-5). The Sink Creek campsite is located a short .2 of a mile from the creek entrance. Look for a small channel marker on the south side of the channel, or follow GPS 29° 33.40,′ W83° 24.10.′ Take time to visit the spring, a short paddle distance upstream. This site also offers hiking potential on forest roads with good photo-op scenic vistas. Beware low tide. Watch out for rocks.

North Pepperfish Keys (Map 15-5). 1.5 miles south from Bowlegs Point. The camping spot is on the west side of the north key. It's not a very nice site because of the narrow piece of high land it sits on. It used to be an old house site and numerous pilings can still be seen in the water and concrete foundation stones on land. This island contains the largest solid grove of prickly pear cactus I've ever seen. They start right behind the campsite and cover the island. There are probably three tent sites that won't put you too close to the cactus. My negative reaction to this site probably came from my expectations. "Pepperfish Keys" is such a neat name. It should be better than it is. There may be a few sites available on South Pepperfish Keys, but we couldn't find any after a cursory look.

Our experience with Pepperfish Keys was negative from the start. The fog had been so thick during the day that we were paddling by compass, and aimed for South Pepperfish for camping for the night. When we got up the next morning, we couldn't see water. The fog was thick and the tide out. We had to wait until almost noon to leave. After we left, we discovered we camped on the North key by mistake. Things cleared up (both physically and mentally) as we left the island. We started netting scallops as we drifted by and got enough for supper that night. We had our first capsize in nine years just south of Pepperfish Keys. One of our party leaned over too far upwind trying to capture one of those elusive scallops and his boat floated out from under him. We pumped out the boat, he jumped back in and we went on. My next trip to this area is going to be better!

There was one bright happening. On the beach at South Pepperfish we saw a flock of about 200 white ibis and 75 to 100 white pelicans feeding and circling with the sun glowing through their wings. With a name like "Pepperfish ...."

Site #11. Horseshoe Beach (Map 15-5). This is another small fishing village with all the usual amenities. There is no beach and no horseshoes, but otherwise it's a pleasant place to restock.

The local convenience store and post office are about a mile up road from the public boat ramp that faces the Gulf. If the tide is in, you can paddle up the canal until it runs out and climb a small bank to save you some walking. If you miss the tide, this is a very muddy area.

I wish our fishing villages were like those old New England villages with picturesque sheds and stone houses. They ain't. Most of Florida's coastal villages are plywood shacks and trailers with a few cement block or wood frame houses thrown in. Ninety percent of the structures are newer than 40 years, or date to the last major storm. Occasionally you can find some well-built old houses or some new giants way up on poles (to meet federal insurance requirements). They're interesting but they're not that interesting. There are one or two hamburger grills on the Gulf side of Horseshoe that sell sandwiches, tackle, and beer and a small restaurant near the convenience store. That was a few years ago. In February 2004, a new luxury condominium was announced. Cost for a Gulf view? $250,000.

Horseshoe Beach Spoil Island (Map 15-5). 0.8 n. miles from Horseshoe Beach on the south side of the channel. This island is about 10 to 15 acres and has been around long enough that the cabbage palms and cedars have grown fairly tall. The west end of the island has a grassy area that may go under water at very high tides but is a pleasant place to set a tent. Inside the island is a sandy place surrounded by cabbage palms and well-protected from the winds. There are also a few sites among the cedars. Ten tents wouldn't overcrowd this island. About 30 black-crowned night herons left the place just as we settled in. I guess that's a good or bad sign.

The approach to the island is best from the north, but the landing is on a beach composed of a mix of oyster shells, rock, and mud. The channel isn't too far away, so even at low tide you can get away from the island with a minimum (for this coast) of mud pulling.

Horseshoe Cove (Map 15-5). 1.5 n. miles from Horseshoe Spoil Island. This is a long, narrow hammock which is part of a county recreation area. Camping isn't allowed as far as I know, but if the spot interests you, ask. The islands south of Horseshoe Beach are privately owned and should be avoided. The next really safe campsite is Butler Island, then Shired Island county park, where an RV and tent campground has been established.

Site #12 Butler Island Campsite (Map 15-5) is located on a peninsula of land south and east of Horseshoe Beach. Paddle around the park, then east south east between Cotton Island and Butler Island. The camp site is on the south side of the island.

6. Shired Island to Clark Island (See Map # 15-6.)

Site #13. Shired Island Campground (Map 15-6). 6 n. miles from Horseshoe Beach Spoil Island. This is a long, narrow strip of land connected to the mainland by marsh grasses. It was an extensive Native American habitation site. The county RV park and campground is on the south end of the island, easily seen from the water. A fee is charged. The island is covered by very large oak trees and the beach area is quite extensive with a lot of interesting shells. There are also some weird fossilized tree roots at the north end.

The water area around the island is composed of numerous oyster bars extending in all different directions and can be very confusing in fog and low tides. Look around for the most convenient boat channel as you come in and mentally mark it for the day you leave. The low tides can give you a lot of trouble here.

Big (Little) Pine Island. 1.5 n. miles from Shired Island. These islands are similar to Shirred Island but have deeper uplands. From this point south to Suwannee, there are no lands legally available for camping. All of this land is part of the Lower Suwannee River National Wildlife Refuge. We received permission to camp when mapping the sites, but others would have to get the same permission to camp this area. (Write Lower Suwannee NWR, Rt. I, Box 1193c, Chiefland, FL 32626.)

Cat Island. 3.5 n. miles from Little Pine Island. This is a true island with the camping sites part of a Native American shell midden in a half moon shape along the west and north side.

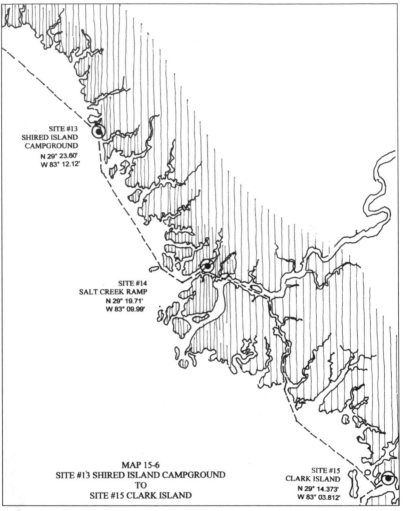

Map # 15-6

Little Bradford Island. 1.5 n. miles from Cat Island on a cut-off from the Suwannee River. The site is a very nice hammock, often used by boaters in the area. It's flat and cleared of most of its brush, under large spreading oaks. There is a narrow beach and a fast-flowing channel next to the site with deep water, 5′ from the beach at low tide. The bank is about 5′ above the water and the beach, 3′ to 4′ wide. At high tide the beach disappears.

This campsite had the largest concentration of no-see-ums I'd ever seen for the winter in Florida. Once the temperature reached the upper 60s, lower 70s, they came OUT. When the wind picked up they left or got down low to the ground. It was strange looking around and not seeing or feeling any and then sitting down to work on dinner and being covered. We dove into the tent for a while and brought about a million in with us. To this day, my tent has a lot of little black squash marks to memorialize that occasion. During the early evening, after the bugs went away with the falling temperature, a manatee came up next to the bank and slowly sauntered on. That's a good sign that the temperatures in the water were still high or he/she would have been upriver in one of the warmer springs.

Site #14. Salt Creek Ramp in the Town of Suwannee (Map 15-6). 2 miles upriver from Little Bradford Island. You can get to the village of Suwannee by going up Salt Creek to the north of town or the Suwannee River to the south. Salt Creek is faster and provides better access. If you want to keep paddling, the creek goes around and comes back out in the Gulf (with a high tide) some 4 or 5 miles later. Suwannee has the same village amenities as the other small villages along the route with the same caveats. There's a public boat ramp on Salt Creek that leads to the main paved road of the town 50' away. Just paddle past the large house with the shock-blue roof about 1/4 mile and you'll see it on the right. It's a steep ramp but the county park is just across the road. The park has water, bathrooms, and covered picnic tables. I asked about camping there and no one seemed to know. If you really need a spot, I'd ask around. Someone will let you camp in a front yard if you look forlorn enough. The village is a nice place to decompress and wait for a pickup. Wash your gear at the park and get a head start on a task that is not one of my favorites. We've been picked up here twice and both times had a long enough wait to clean most of the gear. I liked that.

Suwannee to East Pass (Map 15-6). From Suwannee the Trail continues south along the Levy County coast to Yankeetown. You can paddle out the mouth of Salt Creek and take the Gulf route around the town or take the "inside route" through the town, then south along the east pass of the Suwannee River to the gulf. The freshwater riverine scenery is quite different from the salt marsh coastal environs and you'll enjoy the change of pace. And, if you catch an outgoing tide, the paddle, reinforced by the normal southerly flow of the Suwannee, will be an easy drift. Also, consider spending an extra day or two exploring the land and water trails around the town of Suwannee. Overnight stay at the Pelican's Roost B & B is a treat. It will cost you $75-100 per night, but will be well worth it. Campsites are available at several local marinas. Try Miller's, it's a short walk from the Salt Creek Restaurant. In fact you can paddle there. Look for the signs. If you do spend a day or two, be sure to paddle the Lower Suwannee RWR Canoe/Kayak Trail and rent a bicycle and peddle through a coastal swamp on the Dixie Mainline Trail.

The Lower Suwannee NWR surrounds the town, so there's lots of wildlife, but no camping. Look for alligators, manatees, eagles, ospreys and swallow-tailed kites during the spring and fall. Fishing improves considerably if you're so inclined, and the Lower Suwannee NWR Canoe/Kayak Trail is worth exploring.

The Lower Suwannee NWR, established on April 10, 1979, encompasses more than 52,900 acres in Dixie and Levy Counties, including 20 miles of the Suwannee River. There are three marked paddling trails along Demory Creek: Lock Creek, Shingle Creek, and the Suwannee River. They offer short two-hour paddles, or if paddled in tandem, 3-5 hours of paddling.

"Inside Route" through Suwannee. Paddle back out Salt Creek approximately 500 feet to the first canal on your left (south side of Salt Creek). Go south along this canal around Pelican's Roost B & B, then east and north around the community center park. The canal continues parallel to CR 349, under a culvert bridge for about 1/4 of a mile, then south east, under a second culvert bridge to Demory Creek at the Suwannee River. The total distance from the Salt Creek ramp to the Suwannee River is less than 1 and 1/2 miles. Cross the Suwannee River and continue through Magnesia Pass to East Pass, then south along East Pass another 4 and 1/2 miles to the Gulf of Mexico.

Site #15. Clark Island (Map 15-6). Clark Island is a beautifully wooded crescent spit of land set among fringes of sea grasses in shallow waters, protected by grass islands. It's privately owned, and open to campers for a fee (contact Nature Coast Expeditions LLC, 352 543-6463). It's a little tricky to find. Use GPS coordinates N29° 14.37,' W83° 03.82' to get close. Then look for trees and a shell walkway from the waters edge that leads you through the marsh grass to a cheeki hut built for your comfort. It's primitive, but very scenic. It is also the only place to legally camp between Suwannee and Cedar Key.

7. Clark Island to Kelly Creek
(See Map # 15-7.)

Site #16. Shell Mound (Map 15-7). Shell Mound is a large prehistoric Indian mound in the Lower Suwannee NWR. It has a boardwalk and fishing dock but no other facilities, and camping is not allowed. It's a popular fishing and kayaking spot, perfect for stretching. The shell mound is a short walk from the dock and well worth the effort. It's scenic, historic, and the view from the top of the mound is unique for this part of Florida.

Site #17. Number Four Channel Bridge and the City of Cedar Key (Map 15-7). The public boat ramp at the Number Four Channel Bridge is a convenient pick-up site, and the shortest route from Shell Mound south to Yankeetown, but that's it. Camping is not allowed, parking is limited and there are no other facilities. But it's convenient to SR 24. Tent camping is available nearby at Cedar Key Sunset Isle RV Park (800-810-1103). To get there, about 200 yards before the Number Four bridge, veer south and paddle parallel to the bridge and SR 24 to the second land mass attached to the road. The first land mass about 500' south of the bridge is a private residence. Sunset Isle RV Park is the second land area about 1500' south of the bridge. If the tides are right, it's a short, direct paddle. At low tide, there may not be enough water for a direct route. If this doesn't suit your taste, you can either continue on 10 miles to Site #18 Kelly Creek, or paddle to the public

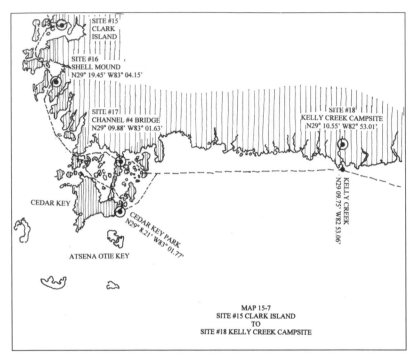

Map # 15-7

beach in town and stay at a motel, B & B, or condominium, of which there are numerous choices. There are also many restaurants, shops, art galleries, and interesting places to visit. Plan an extra day or two into your itinerary. It's worth it.

Cedar Key is the largest (about 1,000 people) and most developed of the villages along the Trail. Its chamber of commerce describes the town as "a quiet island community nestled among many tiny keys on the Gulf Coast of Florida. It's a place where time stands still and allows you to enjoy the unique qualities of this coastal environment. Cedar Key is one of the oldest ports in the state and when Florida's first railroad connected it to the east coast it was a major supplier of seafood and timber products. Today it's a haven for artists and writers who find the unspoiled environment inspirational to their work."

The town itself is a nice touristy place to visit. It is a town, however; you will see many fishing and cruising boats on the weekends, so follow Map 15-7 to the beach at the city park.

Approach it from the south east and miss some of the public marina traffic. In spite of motorboat traffic, the paddling is high quality. A paddle to, around, and through the cut at Otsena Otie Key is a must. And, a very enjoyable day can be spent paddling to other nearby islands and along the many canals and bayous in town. Get a detailed map; it's easy to get lost.

If you choose not to stay a day in Cedar Key, an alternative plan would be to stop at Shell Mound (Site #16) and arrange transport with a local outfitter to the Number Four Channel Bridge by land, put back in at the boat ramp and paddle on to Site #18, Kelly Creek campsite. One outfitter that will provide this service is Ancient Florida Eco-Tours (352-490-5830). Another is Wild Florida Adventures (877-945-3928). There are others; check the Cedar Key and Pure Water Wilderness websites.

Site #18. Kelly Creek Campsite (Map 15-7). The campsite is located approximately 1.2 miles from the mouth of Kelly Creek (GPS N29° 09.75,' W82° 53.06') in the Waccasassa Bay Preserve State Park.

The Waccasassa Bay Preserve State Park contains approximately 34,000 acres on the Gulf of Mexico stretching from Yankeetown on the South to Cedar Key on the north. The preserve, which is home to numerous endangered, threatened, and rare plant and animal species, consists mostly of low wetlands whose primary natural community is the hydric hammock. Vast expanses of tidal marsh border the hydric hammock. Kelly Creek is one of the many tidal waters that meander through the salt marsh community. Turtle Creek is another.

8. Turtle Creek to Yankeetown (See Map # 15-8.)

Site #19. Turtle Creek Campsite (Map 15-8). The Turtle Creek campsite is located approximately 1.5 miles from the mouth of the creek. It is also in the Waccasassa Bay Preserve State Park, where facilities are very limited because protection of the natural resources is the priority. Only low intensity uses such as primitive

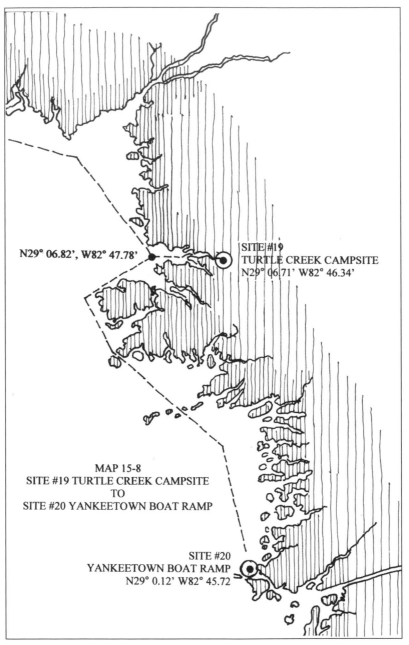

N29° 06.82', W82° 47.78'

SITE #19
TURTLE CREEK CAMPSITE
N29° 06.71' W82° 46.34'

MAP 15-8
SITE #19 TURTLE CREEK CAMPSITE
TO
SITE #20 YANKEETOWN BOAT RAMP

SITE #20
YANKEETOWN BOAT RAMP
N29° 0.12' W82° 45.72

Map # 15-8

camping are allowed and water access is preferred. Limited use (up to 8 people per site) is allowed. Minimum facilities are planned to include designated tent area, fire ring and picnic table. The sites are designated as pack-it-in, pack-it-out only.

Site #20. Yankeetown Boat Ramp (Map 15-8). Paddling out of the mouth of Turtle Creek into Turtle Creek Bay, around Turtle Creek Point and inside South Mangrove Point, the water clears up for the final 6 mile leg to the public boat ramp at the end of Highway 40. Mangrove islands appear, some solid enough to exit your boat and stretch your legs, picnic, fish and enjoy. And, on the weekends, you'll probably encounter motorboats; most are courteous and slow down for paddlers. The public boat ramp is the southern takeout point on the Big Bend Saltwater Paddling Trail. Parking is limited, there are no facilities, and don't plan to camp at this location. However, you can paddle up the Withlacoochee River and find a few private marinas and campgrounds. Paddling the river and its estuary is high quality and worth another day's stay.

Summary

The Big Bend Saltwater Paddling Trail is a special Florida paddling experience because it's so different from the rest of the state. You won't see a high rise condominium anywhere along the 160-mile journey. And, other than a few three-story structures in Cedar Key and elevated residences near and around the few fishing villages, there are very few signs of civilization. No development, no people. It's different and likely to stay that way because the coastline (depending on how it's measured) is almost 90% in public ownership. This mostly undeveloped, low-energy coastal regime belongs to nature. You the intruder are put back in time. Relax. Wind and tides encourage you to take it easy and enjoy the pristine tidal marsh, wading birds, and sea creatures. There are a number of very good campsites, side trips, and villages to visit that will allow you to pick and choose a trip tailored to your needs and preferences.

Beware of the tides and have a good time.

Appendix 1

Constructing a Sea Kayak Seat Back

The following are directions for making a new seat back for your kayak. Because paddlers come in different sizes and shapes, the seat back that comes with the boat may not suit you very well. Some want them higher, some lower, but almost everyone would like some modification. The following is a method for making a seat back that can be varied to fit any size or shape. I like mine higher rather than lower. Though I use an illustration for an Aquaterra Chinook, with a little imagination you can adapt this method to any boat you want. (See the illustration.)

1. Materials. Seat Back: 1/4" Plexiglas, 12" x 14"; two wood pieces 1/2" x 2" x 6-1/2"; six, 3/4" stainless-steel #6 or #8 wood screws; 8" x 10" piece of closed-cell foam for comfort.

2. Sizing. The most frequent complaint I've heard about seat backs is that they're cut too low. I presume this is done to permit a tight closure for the upper part of the skirt and allow for greater upper body movement. For those of us who head to shore when the waves get over 4', the closure of a coated nylon skirt is good enough, and a few extra inches of seat back don't seem to affect a grooved, distance paddle stroke. If you're going to do big wave surfing or ocean crossings, maybe you need to stick with the low seat back. My seat back is 14" high and seems to work for all people sizes from 5'1" to 6'4". I round the top edges for safety and cut off the bottom corners so it will fit easily in the groove of the Chinook™ seat. Your seat back width will depend on the boat you paddle, but 12" seems to work fine.

3. Cutting, drilling, and sanding. You can cut Plexiglas with a hand or power saw with little difficulty. Any metal drill will work

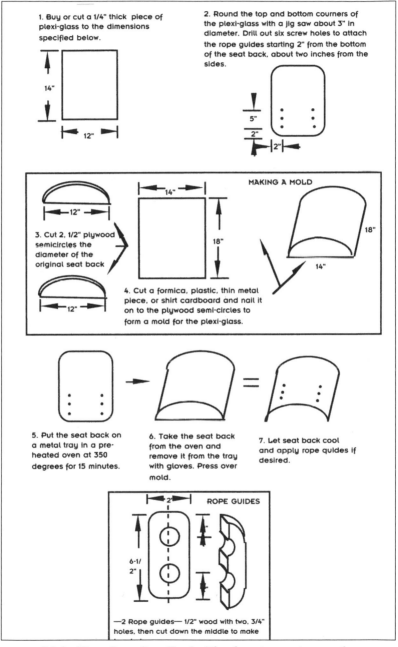

1. Buy or cut a 1/4" thick piece of plexi-glass to the dimensions specified below.

14"

12"

2. Round the top and bottom courners of the plexi-glass with a jig saw about 3" in diameter. Drill out six screw holes to attach the rope guides starting 2" from the bottom of the seat back, about two inches from the sides.

5"

2"

2"

MAKING A MOLD

3. Cut 2, 1/2" plywood semicircles the diameter of the original seat back

12"

12"

14"

18"

18"

14"

4. Cut a formica, plastic, thin metal piece, or shirt cardboard and nail it on to the plywood semi-circles to form a mold for the plexi-glass.

5. Put the seat back on a metal tray in a pre-heated oven at 350 degrees for 15 minutes.

6. Take the seat back from the oven and remove it from the tray with gloves. Press over mold.

7. Let seat back cool and apply rope guides if desired.

ROPE GUIDES

2"

6-1/2"

—2 Rope guides— 1/2" wood with two, 3/4" holes, then cut down the middle to make

Make Your Own Seat Back. *The above instructions are for an Aquaterra Chinook but can be adapted to most boats.*

well. Sand the rough edges with 100 to 150 grit sandpaper. If you've had no experience with either Plexiglas or tools, practice on some scrap before you start, to get the feel of the material.

4. Shaping. The nicest thing about Plexiglas is how easy it is to shape into interesting and comfortable curves. If you preheat your household oven to 350° and place your cut and sized piece of Plexiglas on a cookie sheet for 15 minutes, it can be bent almost any way you want. The longer you leave it in, the greater the flexibility. Fifteen minutes in the oven is about what you need for single curve seat bending. Too much heat can turn it into jello. Once you take it out of the oven (handle with heat gloves or pot holders), you can bend it to shape or press it over a mold you've constructed. If it doesn't turn out like you want it, put it back in the oven on a flat surface and start over when it straightens out. The Plexiglas is pliable as long as it's hot. When it cools off it will stay in place. You can still flex the Plexiglas about 1/2″ or so, but it will rebound to its previous shape. It can be reheated and reshaped if you want.

5. Molds. If you want to be sure that your seat back has the right curve, you need to build a mold. Though it may take more time than the rest of the project, it's usually worth it. Since the mold is reusable, it can be passed around to a lot of friends. The one shown in the illustration is very simple. Its only purpose is to do a single curve along the vertical axis. I used the existing seat back as a template to get the curve line and cut out two pieces of plywood at a slightly more extreme curvature because the Plexiglas will pull away from the mold a little. I then used a scrap piece of Formica and nailed it to the plywood. You can probably use anything that will flex and can stand heat of 350°. I think shirt cardboard would work once, but I'm not sure.

6. Rope guides. Some kayaks have adjustable seat backs that use ropes or cords for tension or location controls. The guides keep the ropes in the correct position and the seat back from falling out when the boat is upside down (for traveling or storage, since no one rolls sea kayaks?). I made my first guides from Plexiglas scraps that I cut off the seat back during construction. Some I slued on and some I attached with screws. The glue didn't hold and the screws fractured the Plexiglas. Since then I switched to non-rotting wood like cypress or cedar. After drilling holes through the Plexiglas, it's easy to attach the wooden guides with stainless-steel wood screws. If these don't work, just drill two holes and run some insulated #12 wires through and make a loop around the ropes.

7. Cushioning. I use a closed-cell foam like Ensolite because I happened to have it around and it won't soak up water. Contact cement seems to work best for attaching the foam, but any waterproof glue that won't dissolve the foam or plastic will do.

8. Cost. You should be able to buy the Plexiglas for under $10 at a local glass or plastic specialty store, cut to size. Ensolite pads can be purchased in the camping section of many discount stores for around $10. Since that's enough foam for four seat backs, you could buy with friends.

Appendix 2

Paddle Suspension Rig

The illustration on the next page gives a general view of the paddle suspension rig that I saw being used by a Vietnam war veteran who had major arm and shoulder problems. The basic idea is to find a way to take the weight of the paddle away from the paddler and put it on a mechanical device that doesn't kill him or her. Construction of this rig will require some general knowledge of PVC plumbing pipes and the ability to use a measuring tape, saw, and drill. Below is a more specific drawing.

Start by acquiring your materials. Cut each piece into the proper length (you may need some modifications if the main paddler is a lot smaller or taller than average). The diagram fails to show the aluminum tube that runs through the center of the PVC pipe for stiffness. This tube is approximately 1-1/8″ outside diameter and fits inside the 1-1/4″ PVC. The tubing can be purchased at any hardware store or do-it-yourself place. Try the tubes in the store and make sure they fit. If the Tee is not too tight, one long piece can fit all the way from the bottom to the top.

Once the material is collected and cut, assemble the PVC and aluminum tubes and glue the PVC together using the usual PVC solvent and glue. Glue the caps on the ends.

Drill holes through the top of the upright end of the extended arm and fasten the eye bolts. These should be stainless steel, brass, or cheap steel (if you don't mind replacing them often).

Cut a hole in the boat just behind the cockpit and screw in a through-the-hull fitting (thingy) whose inside diameter hole is just large enough for the PVC. You can get these at any boat hardware place or through the boat catalogs. They come in chrome-plated brass, nylon, or plastic and are composed of two pieces that screw together with various diameters and flange sizes. They're often used as plumbing fixtures or deck drains. You should seal the parts

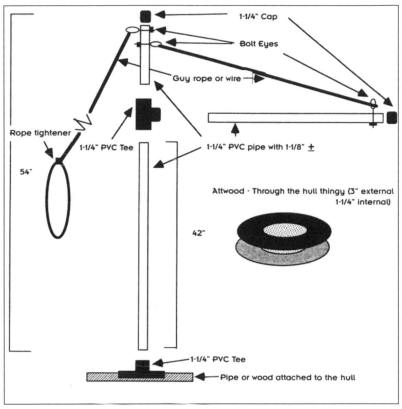

Paddle Suspension Rig

with good caulking for a watertight seal. The one I use is made by Attwood, but there are lots of others on the market. If you have to buy one that's bigger than you want, just wrap some duct tape around the upright pipe or figure out a more permanent fix. I slid a 1″ segment of 1-1/2″ thinwall PVC over the pipe for a nice fit.

The most difficult construction will be the connector at the bottom of the upright pipe that anchors the system to the bottom of the boat. My Chinook came with a plastic-covered steel pipe that runs down the center of the boat. I just cut the PVC Tee lengthwise and bolted it onto the pipe with the flange connector sticking up. I then drilled a hole through both the upright pipe and the flange and stuck a nail through to hold the upright pipe in place. This allowed me to pull the nail and the whole rig out when

I didn't need to use it. If you don't have a pipe in the bottom of a "Tupperware" boat, you may have to find one, or build a wooden platform that will stay in place. If you have a fiberglass boat, you may have to glass in a cut Tee or build a plate similar to a mast step to accomplish the same purpose.

Once the rig is constructed, you will need to attach the guy ropes to the top of the upright, the end of the extension arm, and the back grab loop. You can use parachute or tent cord and tent tighteners to get the required tension to make sure the rig stays in place. Loop a bungee cord over the extension arm, attach to the paddle, and off you go. If this last step is a problem, look for a paddle safety ring (or shower curtain ring) that you can attach to the paddle (when broken apart) and tie the bungee to the ring. I sewed a system with a Fastex buckle that allows height adjustments and quick take down if trouble occurs.

If you intend to travel with the rig only part of the time, buy a good cork from your local tackle store, drill a hole in the middle, attach a string, tie the string to the boat, and plug the cork in when needed.

Appendix 3
A List of Kayak Books

The following is a short list of more recent publications that could be of interest to sea kayakers in Florida. It includes some freshwater as well as saltwater information. Many of these will be available from kayak dealers and sporting goods stores, though the selection will vary and often will be spotty.

A Canoeing and Kayaking Guide to the Streams of Florida, Vol. I: North and Central Peninsula and Panhandle. Carter, Elizabeth F., and Pearce, John L. Menasha Ridge Press, 1986. 216pp.

A Canoeing and Kayaking Guide to the Streams of Florida, Vol. II: Central and South Peninsula. Glaros, Lou, and Sphar, Doug. Menasha Ridge Press, 1987. 136pp.

Eskimo Rolling, 3rd Ed. Hutchinson, Derek. Chester, Connecticut: Globe Pequot Press, 1999. 134pp.

Fundamentals of Kayak Navigation, 3rd Ed. Burch, David. Globe Pequot Press, 1999. 342pp.

Hooper Bay Kayak Construction, Vol. 53. Zimmerly, David W. Ottawa: Canadian Museum of Civilization, 2001. 107pp.

Hypothermia, Frostbite and Other Cold Injuries. Wilkerson, James ed. Seattle: The Mountaineers, 1993. 150pp.

Kayak Cookery, 2nd Ed. Daniel, Linda. Menasha Ridge Press, 1997. 208pp.

Kayaking Puget Sound, the San Juans and Gulf Islands: 45 Trips on the Northwest's Inland Waters. Washburn, Randel. The Mountaineers, 1990. 222pp.

Paddle Routes of Western Washington: 50 Flatwater Trips for Canoe and Kayak, 2nd Ed. Huser, Verne. The Mountaineers, 2000. 240pp.

Performance Kayaking. U'Ren, Stephen B. Harrisburg: Stackpole Books, 1990. 184pp.

Sea Kayaking: A Manual for Long-Distance Touring, Rev. Ed. Dowd, John. Seattle: University of Washington Press, 1997. 304pp.

The Bark Canoes and Skin Boats of North America, 2nd Ed. Adney, Chapelle, and E.T. Adney. Washington D.C.: Smithsonian Institution, 1993. 242pp.

The Canoeing and Kayaking Instruction Manual. Gullion, Laurie. American Canoe Association, 1993. 112pp.

The Coastal Kayakers Manual, 3rd Ed. Washburne, Randel. Globe Penquot Press, 1998. 256pp.

The Essential Sea Kayaker, 2nd Ed. Seidman, David. Camden, Maine: International Marine Publishing, 2000. 160pp.

The First Crossing of Greenland. Nansen, Fridtjof. University Press of the Pacific, 2001. 486pp.

Wilderness Medicine: Beyond First Aid, 5th Ed. Forgey, William. Globe Pequot Press, 1999. 256pp.

Wood and Canvas Kayak Building. Putz, George. International Marine Publishing, 1990. 133pp.

Magazines of Interest

Atlantic Coastal Kayaker. P.O. Box 520, Ipswich, MA 01938. 978-356-6112. www.ackayak.com

Canoe and Kayak. 10526 N.E. Suite 3, Kirkland, WA 98033. 425-827-6363 or 1-800-692-2663. www.canoekayak.com

Paddler Magazine. P.O. Box 775450, Steamboat Springs, CO 80487. 970-879-1450 or 888-774-7554. www.paddlermagazine.com

Sea Kayaker. 7001 Seaview Avenue N.W. Suite 135, Seattle, WA 98127. 206-789-9536. www.seakayakermag.com

Appendix 4 - Camping List

Boat Clothing
Polypro underwear
Paddling sweater
Paddling jacket – waterproof,
 one that breathes, if possible
Tie hat for sun protection
Gloves for paddling

Sweatpants and sweatshirt for bug protection
Capilene medium-weight shirt
Lycra pants for sun protection
Bandana
Rain pants and jacket
Bathing suit

Camp Clothing
Camp shoes
Short pants
T-shirts
Belt

Warm jacket or vest
Long shirt (light)
Wool-Polypro socks
Underwear

Long pants
Long shirt (heavy)
Warm hat
Mosquito hat

Camping
Tent
Pillow/case
Tarp for campsite
Towels
Flashlight, batteries, bulb

Sleeping pad
Lantern
Water bag and bottles
Biodegradable soap
Candle

Sleeping bag
Knife, multipurpose
Water filter
Toilet paper and shovel
Sewing kit

Cooking
Stove
Pots
Plate, bowl, cup
Matches, lighter
Oyster knife

Fuel
Spoon, fork
Ziplock bags
Dish towel
Scrubber

Grill
Pot lifter
Garbage bags
Can opener
Kitchen kit

Miscellaneous
Sunglasses
Weather radio
Chair

Whistle
Extra rope, twine
Handiwipes

Two-way radio
Cameras, binoculars
Cellular phone/GPS

Boating
Paddle
Skirt
Bilge pump
Sail
Mask and fins
Bow line

Spare paddle
Dry bags
Foam feet pad
Anchor
Fishing equipment
Sponge

Flotation (storage)
Compass
Flares
Life vest
Cast net
Whistle

Safety
Anti-bacterial ointment
Asprin, Tylenol
Antacid
2nd Skin/tape
Sunscreen

Suture kit
Dental kit
Anti-motion sickness pills
Cortisone cream
Liniment

Tweezers, scalpel
Bandages, gauze
Ace bandage
Chapstick
Insect repellant

Navigation
Road map
Tide tables

Coastal maps
Map cases

Quad maps

Food Planning

Monday
  Breakfast _____
  Lunch _____
  Dinner _____

Tuesday
  Breakfast _____
  Lunch _____
  Dinner _____

Wednesday
  Breakfast _____
  Lunch _____
  Dinner _____

Thursday
  Breakfast _____
  Lunch _____
  Dinner _____

Friday
  Breakfast _____
  Lunch _____
  Dinner _____

Saturday
  Breakfast _____
  Lunch _____
  Dinner _____

Sunday
  Breakfast _____
  Lunch _____
  Dinner _____

Staples

Limes	Salt	Pepper	Garlic	Mix of spices
Cheese	Butter Buds	Jelly	Hot sauce	Tea
Carrots	Pita/bagles	Peanuts	Wine	Fresh fruit
Cocoa	Apples/oranges	Peanut butter	Olive oil	Hot spiced apple
Bananas	Dry milk	Sweet onion	Coffee	Gorp (Trail mix)
	Mangoes			

Small packs: mayo, taco sauce, relish. barbeque sauce, mustard, catsup, tartar sauce, duck sauce, sugar

Appendix 5

Boat Liveries, Outfitters, and Associations

Florida Sea Kayaking Association. FSKA is a network of paddlers who love the sport of kayaking. www.fska.org

Panhandle

Adventurers Unlimited. 8974 Tomahawk Landing Road, Milton, FL 32570. 850-623-6197 or 1-800-239-6864. www.adventurersunlimited.com

Blackwater Canoe Rental and Sales. 6974 Deaton Bridge Road, Milton, FL 32583. 850-623-0235 or 1-800-967-6789. www.blackwatercanoe.com

Big Bend

Canoe Shop. 1115-B W. Orange Avenue, Tallahassee, FL 32310. 850-576-5335. www.paddlenorthflorida.com

Paddle Tallahasee is a public forum open to everyone interested in canoeing and kayaking. It offers a wealth of information to Tallahassee-area kayak and canoe paddlers. www.paddletally.org

T.N.T. Hideaway. 6527 Coastal Highway, Saint Marks, FL 32355. 850-925-6412. www.tnthideawaycanoe-kayak-rental.com

Wild Florida Adventures. P.O. Box 6262, Williston, FL 32696. 352-528-3984 or 877-945-3928. www.wild-florida.com/index.shtml

Northeast

Costal Kayaks Co. 4255 A1A South, St. Augustine, FL 32080. 904-471-4144. No website available

Outdoor Adventures. 1625 Emerson Street, Jacksonville, FL 32207. 904-393-9030. No website available

West Central

Agua Azul Kayaks. 343 Causeway Boulevard, Dunedin, FL 34698. 727-738-4576. No website available

By the Bay Outfitters. 520 Blackburn Point Road, Osprey, FL 34229. 941-966-3937. www.kayakflorida.com

Canoe Country Outfitters. 6493 54th Avenue North, St. Petersburg, FL 33709. 1-800-330-1550. www.canoecountryfl.com

Canoe Escape, Inc. 9335 E. Fowler Avenue, Thonotosassa, FL 33592. 813-986-2067. www.canoeescape.com

Canoe Outpost, Little Manatee. 18001 U.S. 301 S., Wimauma, FL 33598. 813-634-2228. www.canoeoutpost.com

Canoe Outpost, Peace River. 2816 NW C.R. 661, Arcadia, FL 34266. 1-800-268-0083. www.canoeoutpost.com/peace.html

Ray's Canoe Hide-Away. 1247 Hagle Park Road, Bradenton, FL 34212. 941-747-3909. www.rayscanoehideaway.com

Snook Haven Retreat. 5000 E. Venice Avenue, Venice, FL 34292. 941-485-7221. www.venice-fla.com/snookhaven/

Sweetwater Kayaks. 10000 Gandy Boulevard, St. Petersburg, FL 33702. 727-570-4844.www.sweetwaterkayaks.com

North Central

Adventure Outpost. 815 NW Santa Fe Boulevard, High Springs, FL 32643. 386-454-0611. www.adventureoutpost.net

Canoe Outpost, Santa Fe. P.O. Box 592, High Springs, FL 32655. 386-454-2050. www.santaferiver.com

Canoe Outpost, Suwannee. 2461 95th Drive, Live Oak, FL 32060. 1-800-428-4147. www.canoeoutpost.com/Suwannee/

Central

Aardvark's Florida Kayak Company. 425-B N. Citrus Avenue, Crystal River, FL 34429. 352-795-5650. www.floridakayak company. com/

Brasington's Trail Shop. 2331 N.W. 13th Street, Gainesville, FL 32609. 352-372-0521. www.ebrasingtons.com/home/home.php

Katie's Wekiva River Landing. 190 Katie's Cove, Sanford, FL 32771. 407-628-1482. www.ktland.com

Old Spanish Sugar Mill. P.O. Box 879, Altoona, FL 32702, 904-985-5644. No website available

Oklawaha Outpost. 15260 N.E. 152nd Place, Fort McCoy, FL 32134. 866-236-4606. www.outpostresort.com/home.html

Sundowner Kayak Adventures. Locations throughout Central Florida. 352-489-9797. sundowner-kayak-adventures.com/

Southwest

Canoe Outpost, Peace River. 2816 N.W. County Road 661, Arcadia, FL 34266. 863- 494-1215. www.canoeoutpost.com/peace.html

Canoe Safari. 3020 N.W. County Road 661, Arcadia, FL 34266. 863-494-7865. www.canoesafari.com

Estero River Tackle, Kayak & Canoe Outfitters. 20991 S. Tamiami Trail, Estero, FL 33928. 239-992-4050. www.esteroriver outfitters.com/

Grande Tours Eco-Tours and Kayaking. 12575 Placida Road, Placida, FL 33946. 941-697-8825. www.grandctours.com/

Gulf Area Sea Paddlers (GASP). This is an organization for sea kayakers interested in paddling the Gulf of Mexico and Caribbean areas. www.gasp-seakayak.org

Gulf Coast Kayak. 4530 Pine Island Road, Matlacha, FL 33993. 239-283-1125. www.gulfcoastkayak.com

Silent Sports Outfitters. 2301 Tamiami Trail, Nokomis, FL 34275. 941-966-5477. www.adventuresinflorida.net/silentsportsout fitters.htm

Southeast

Adventure Times Kayaks. 521 Northlake Boulevard, North Palm Beach, FL 33408. 1-888-kayak-fl. www.adventuretimes.com

Atlantic Coast Kayak Company. 1869 S. Dixie Highway, Pompano Beach, FL 33060. 954-781-0073. www.atlantic coastkayak.com

Canoe Outfitters of Florida. 9060 W. Indiantown Road, Jupiter, FL 33478. 561-746-7053. www.canoes-kayaks-florida.com

Southern Exposure Sea Kayaks. 18487 S.E. Federal Highway, Tequesta, FL 33469. 561-575-4530. No website available

Waterways Kayak. 1406 North Ocean Drive, Hollywood, FL 33019. 954-921-8944. No website available

South Central

Palmdale Campground, Inc. Highway 27, Palmdale, FL 33944. 941-675-1852. No website available

South

Florida Bay Outfitters. 104050 Overseas Highway, Key Largo, FL 33037. 305-451-3018. www.kayakfloridakeys.com

Florida Keys Backcountry Adventures. 6810 Front Street, Key West, FL 33040. 305-296-0362. www.keywest-fl.com/tom1.htm

Florida Keys Kayaks and Canoes by Scarlet Ibis. Contact for tour locations. 305-872-0032. keys-kayak-canoe-tours.com/canoe.htm

Ibis Tours, Everglades. P.O. Box 208, Pelham, NY 10803. 1-800-525-9411. www.ibistours.com

Mangrove Coast Seakayaks and Canoes. 5794 Commerce Lane, S. Miami, FL 33143. 305-663-3364. No website available

Mosquito Coast. 310 Duval Street, Key West, FL 33040. 305-294-7178. mosquitocoast.net

Mothership Sea Kayaking with Fishabout. 105 Palm Lane, Islamorada, FL 33036. 305-853-0741. www.fishabout.org

North American Canoes Tours, Inc. 107 Camellia Street, P.O. Box 5038, Everglades City, FL 34139. 239-695-3299. www.ever gladesadventures.com

Ocean Paddler South. Marathon, FL 33050. 305-743-0131. No website available

Sea Kayak Vacations by Voyagers Kayak Center. P.O. Box 500281, 73 Coco Plum Drive, Marathon, FL 33050. 305-743-0887. www.raftvoyagers.com

Appendix 6

Everglades National Park Campsite Map & Chart

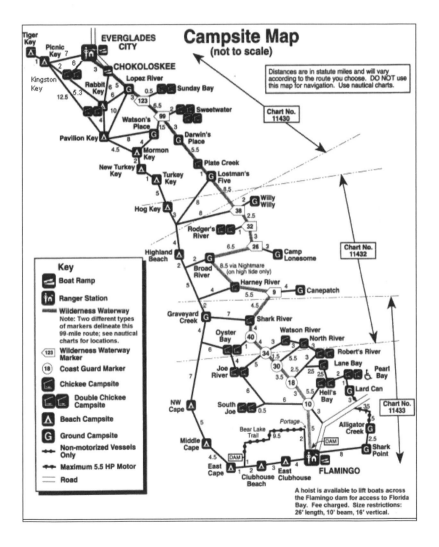

Campsite Name	Type of Site	# People	# Parties	# Nights	Toilet	Table	Dock
Alligator Creek	Ground	8	3	2			
Broad River	Ground	10	3	2	yes	yes	yes
Camp Lonesome	Ground	10	3	3	yes	yes	yes
Canepatch	Ground	12	4	3	yes	yes	yes
Cape Sable, East	Beach	60	15	7			
Cape Sable, Middle	Beach	60	15	7			
Cape Sable, NW	Beach	36	9	7			
Carl Ross Key	Beach	9	3	2			
Clubhouse Beach	Beach	24	4	3			
Darwin's Place	Ground	8	2	3	yes	yes	
East Clubhouse Beach	Beach	24	4	3			
Ernest Coe***	Ground	8	1	3			
Graveyard Creek	Ground	12	4	3	yes	yes	
Harney River	Chickee	6	1	1	yes		yes
Hell's Bay	Chickee	6/6	1/1	1	yes		yes
Highland Beach	Beach	24	4	3			
Hog Key**	Beach	8	2	2			
Ingraham***	Ground	8	1	3			
Joe River	Chickee	6/6	1/1	1	yes		yes
Kingston Key	Chickee	4/4	1/1	1	yes		yes
Lane Bay	Chickee	6	1	1	yes		yes
Lard Can	Ground	10	4	2	yes		
Little Rabbit Key	Ground	12	4	2	yes	yes	yes
Lopez River	Ground	12	3	2	yes	yes	
Lostman's Five	Ground	10	2	2	yes		yes
Mormon Key	Beach	12	2	3			
New Turkey Key	Beach	10	2	2	yes		
North Nest Key	Beach	25	7	7	yes		yes
North River	Chickee	6	1	1	yes		yes
Oyster Bay	Chickee	6/6	1/1	1	yes		yes
Pavillion Key	Beach	20	4	3	yes		
Pearl Bay****	Chickee	6/6	1/1	1	yes		yes
Picnic Key	Beach	16	3	3	yes		
Plate Creek	Chickee	6	1	1	yes		yes
Rabbit Key	Beach	8	2	2	yes		
Roberts River	Chickee	6/6	1/1	1	yes		yes
Rodgers River	Chickee	6/6	1/1	1	yes		yes
Shark Point**	Ground	8	1	3	*		
Shark River	Chickee	6	1	1	yes		yes
South Joe River	Chickee	6/6	1/1	1	yes		yes
Sunday Bay	Chickee	6/6	1/1	1	yes		yes
Sweetwater	Chickee	6/6	1/1	1	yes		yes
Tiger Key	Beach	12	3	3			
Turkey Key	Beach	12	3	3			
Watson's Place	Ground	20	5	2	yes		yes
Watson River	Chickee	6	1	1	yes	yes	yes
Willy Willy	Ground	10	3	3	yes	yes	yes

      * No toilet facilities - bringing portable toilet recommended.
    ** Shallow water approach; recommended for canoes/kayaks only.
  *** Ernest Coe and Ingraham are accessible on foot or bicycle only.
**** The Pearl Bay Chickee is accessible to people with mobility impairments.
     It features handrails, a canoe dock, and an accessible chemical toilet.

Everglades Campsite Chart

Index

The Exploring Wild series: A series of field guides, each with information on all the parks, preserves, and natural areas in its region, including wildlife to look for and best time of year to visit.

Exploring Wild North Florida by Gil Nelson. From the Suwannee River to the Atlantic shore, and south to include the Ocala National Forest. ISBN 1-56164-091-3 (pb)

Exploring Wild Northwest Florida by Gil Nelson. The Florida Panhandle, from the Perdido River in the west to the Suwannee River in the east. ISBN 1-56164-086-7 (pb)

Exploring Wild South Florida by Susan D. Jewell. The third edition includes over 40 new natural areas and covers Broward, Collier, Dade, Hendry, Lee, Monroe, and Palm Beach Counties. ISBN 1-56164-125-1 (pb)

Best Backroads of Florida, Volumes 1–3 by Douglas Waitley. For vacationers and residents who want to catch a glimpse of the Florida of yesteryear, these books offer single-day backroads tours on Florida's little-traveled byways. Get out of the car to enjoy beautiful picnic areas, lake and river cruises, airboat rides, snorkeling and scuba diving, and biking and hiking through the beauty of Florida's land. Volume 1: The Heartland (central Florida), ISBN 1-56164-189-8 (pb); Volume 2: Coasts, Glades, and Groves (south Florida), ISBN 1-56164-232-0 (pb); Volume 3: Beaches and Hills (north Florida), ISBN 1-56164-283-5 (pb)

The Florida Night Sky by Elinor De Wire. A starting point for those who want to learn the Florida night sky and enjoy its treasures as well as a helpful reference for serious amateur astronomers. Learn where Florida fits into the grand picture of the organized universe. ISBN 1-56164-238-X (hb)

Seashore Plants of Florida and the Caribbean by David W. Nellis. A full-color guide to the flora of nearshore environments, including complete characteristics of each plant as well as ornamental, medicinal, ecological, and other aspects. Suitable for both backyard gardeners and serious naturalists. ISBN 1-56164-026-3 (hb); 1-56164-056-5 (pb)

Florida's Birds: A Handbook and Reference by Herbert W. Kale II and David S. Maehr. Illustrated by Karl Karalus. This fully illustrated guide to identification, enjoyment, and protection of Florida's varied and beautiful population of birds identifies and discusses more than 325 species, with information on distinguishing marks, habitat, season, and distribution. ISBN 0-910923-67-1 (hb); 0-910923-68-X (pb)